Water Safety Plans: Book 4
IRA-WDS Software and Manual for
Risk Assessment of Contaminant Intrusion
into Water Distribution Systems

Water Safety Plans: Book 4

IRA-WDS Software and Manual for Risk Assessment of Contaminant Intrusion into Water Distribution Systems

Kalanithy Vairavamoorthy, Sunil D. Gorantiwar,
Jimin Yan & Harshal M. Galgale

Water, Engineering and Development Centre
Loughborough University
2006

Water, Engineering and Development Centre,
Loughborough University,
Leicestershire, LE11 3TU, UK

© WEDC, Loughborough University, 2006

ISBN 13 Paperback: 978 1 84380 103 0
ISBN Ebook: 9781788533706
Book DOI: http://dx.doi.org/10.3362/9781788533706

A catalogue record for this book is available from the British Library.

A reference copy of this publication is also available online at:
http://www.lboro.ac.uk/wedc/publications/

Vairavamoorthy, K., Gorantiwar, S. D.,
Yan, J. M., and Galgale, H. M., (2006)
Water Safety Plans: Book 4
IRA-WDS Software and Manual for Risk Assessment of
Contaminant Intrusion into Water Distribution Systems
WEDC, Loughborough University, UK

WEDC (The Water, Engineering and Development Centre) at Loughborough University in the UK is one of the world's leading institutions concerned with education, training, research and consultancy for the planning, provision and management of physical infrastructure for development in low- and middleincome countries.

This edition is reprinted and distributed by Practical Action Publishing.
Since 1974, Practical Action Publishing has published and disseminated books and information in support of international development work throughout the world. Practical Action Publishing trades only in support of its parent charity objectives and any profits are covenanted back to Practical Action (Charity Reg. No. 247257, Group VAT Registration No. 880 9924 76).

This document is an output from a project funded by the UK
Department for International Development (DFID)
for the benefit of low-income countries.
The views expressed are not necessarily those of DFID.

Designed at WEDC

About the authors

Kalanithy Vairavamoorthy
(k.vairavamoorthy@unesco-ihe.org) Currently chair for Sustainable Urban Infrastructure Systems in UNESCO, IHE, Delft, the Netherlands and previously a senior lecturer in the Water Engineering Development Centre (WEDC) at Loughborough University. He worked for South Bank University, London, from 1993 to 2002 and was head of the Water Development Research Unit within the Faculty of the Built Environment. He has an MSc degree and PhD in civil engineering from Imperial College, London. He has expertise in the design, operation and maintenance of urban water distribution systems. In particular, he has experience in researching and developing innovative solutions to water supply systems that operate under water shortage scenarios. He has also acted as a consultant on many projects for both UK water companies and overseas clients. More recently he has advised Indian water authorities on the management of intermittent water supplies, implementation of unaccounted for water action plans, leak detection and other related issues.

Sunil D. Gorantiwar
(sdgorantiwar@rediffmail.com) Associate professor and research engineer at the All India Co-ordinated Research Project on Optimisation of Groundwater Utilisation (ICAR) in the Department of Irrigation and Drainage Engineering, Mahatma Phule Agricultural University, Rahuri, India since 1985. Currently he is an academic visitor to the Water Engineering and Development Centre (WEDC), Loughborough University. He has an MTech degree in water resources development and management from IIT, Kharagpur, India and a PhD in civil engineering from Loughborough University, Loughborough, UK. He has expertise in water management of irrigation schemes in developing counties, micro-irrigation methods, optimum utilization of surface and groundwater, urban water related infrastructures and risk-based modelling.

Jimin Yan

(j.yan@lboro.ac.uk) A research scholar in the Water Engineering and Development Centre, Department of Civil Engineering, Loughborough University. He has an MSc degree in civil engineering from Harbin Institute of Technology (HIT), China. He has expertise in hydraulic and water quality modelling of water distribution systems, underground water asset management and unaccounted for water (UFW) management.

Harshal Galgale

(H.Galgale@lboro.ac.uk) A research scholar in the Water Engineering Development Centre, Department of Civil Engineering, Loughborough University. He has completed a MTech degree specializing in irrigation and drainage engineering at Mahatma Phule Agricultural University, Rahuri, India. After his masters he worked for a year at the National Environmental Engineering Research Institute (NEERI), Nagpur, India and Indian Agricultural Research Institute (IARI), New Delhi, India for six months. He was involved in environmental impact assessment studies using Remote Sensing and Geographical Information Systems (GIS) techniques at NEERI and in the design and development of a model for spatial prediction of crop yields on regional scales at IARI. He has expertise in the field of GIS, Remote Sensing and hydrological modelling.

Acknowledgements

The financial support of the UK Department for International Development (DFID) is gratefully acknowledged. The authors would also like to thank those who have contributed to the development of these guidelines.

KAKTOS Consult, Hyderabad, India
India Institute of Technology (IIT), Chennai, India
Guntur Municipal Corporation, Municipal Corporation of Hyderabad, India
Public Health Engineering Department of Guntur, India

Finally, the authors wish to acknowledge Dr Guy Howard, DFID, Bangladesh and Dr Sam Godfrey, UNICEF, India for their intellectual input; Ian Smout, Director, WEDC for his constructive suggestions; Mukund G. Shinde, Li Huipeng and Yibo Shen, Research Scholars, WEDC for testing IRA-WDS; and Rod Shaw, Sue Plummer and Karen Betts of the WEDC Publications Office.

Who should read this book

This book has been written specifically for practitioners involved in the operation, maintenance and management of piped water distribution systems in urban areas of developing countries. These practitioners include engineers, planners, managers, and water professionals involved in the monitoring, control and rehabilitation of water distribution networks.

This book is a manual for using the developed software, IRA-WDS (Improved Risk Assessment for Water Distribution System), a Geographical Information System (GIS) that aids in evaluating the risk of deterioration of the water distribution network of a water supply system. The manual is a structured document and explains a step-by-step procedure for using the IRA-WDS, with examples.

How to use this book

The software IRA-WDS has been developed to evaluate risks to piped water distribution systems of urban areas in developing countries. This manual enables the use of this software. The software consists of three models, namely the Contaminant Ingress Model, Pipe Condition Assessment Model and Risk Assessment Model. The IRA-WDS is designed to use these models together or individually. This manual provides a step-by-step procedure for using these models and obtaining results. Book 3, also developed in this series, should be used along with the software and this manual. This will enable readers to understand and analyse their results.

How does this book fit into the overall guidelines?

This book is Book 4 in the guidelines series developed for Project KaR R8029, Improved Risk Assessment and Management for Piped Urban Water Supplies. It provides details of how to use IRA-WDS, a Geographical Information System (GIS) based software that estimates the risk of contaminant intrusion into water distribution systems from sewers and foul surface water bodies. The technical background to IRA-WDS is presented in Book 3, and readers are encouraged to read Book 3 prior to reading this one. It is also important to recognize that to use IRA-WDS, institutions and authorities responsible for water management need to be committed to the collection and maintenance of data and to developing technical expertise. Therefore, it is recommended that users should also read Book 2 and consider the implementation of IRA-WDS in light of that document's content.

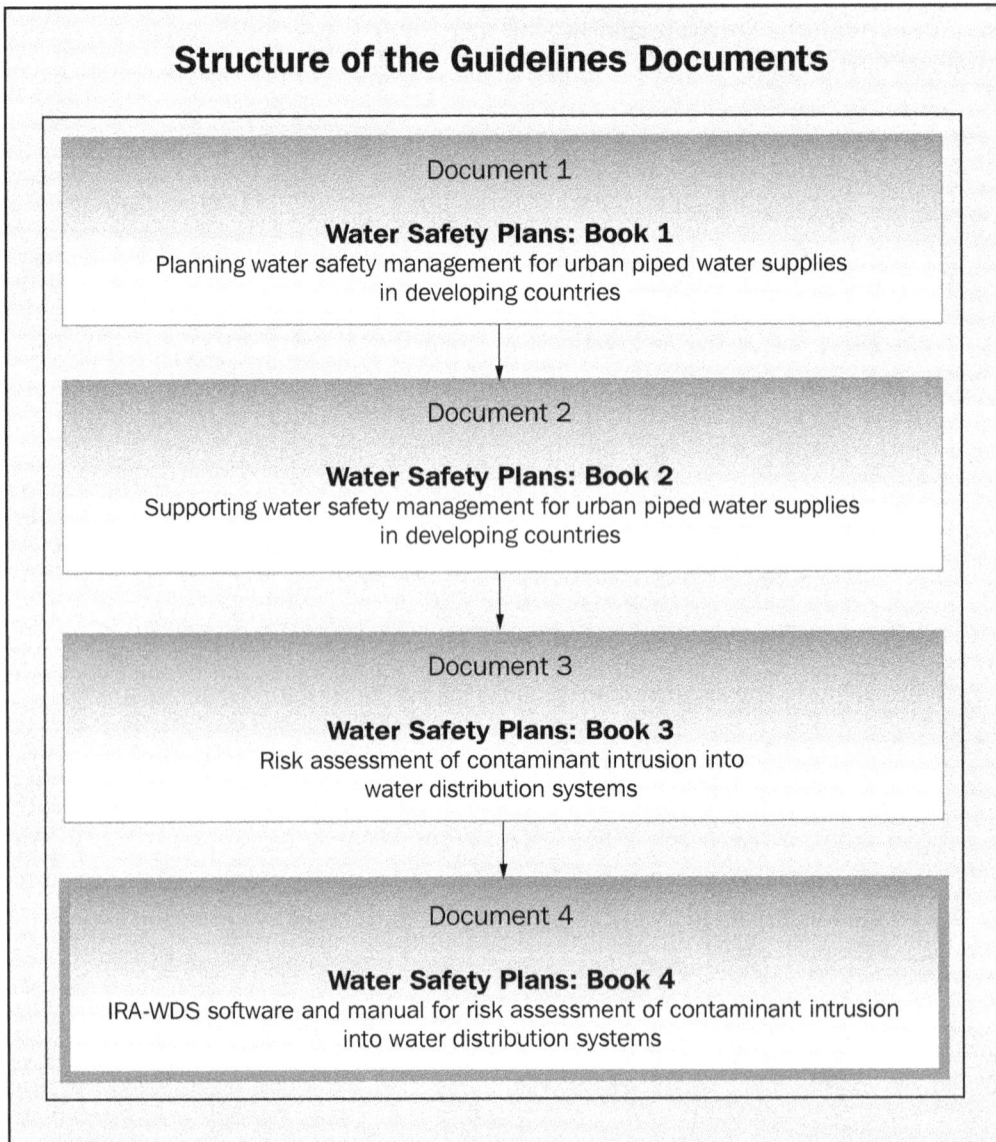

Structure of the Guidelines Documents

Document 1

Water Safety Plans: Book 1
Planning water safety management for urban piped water supplies in developing countries

Document 2

Water Safety Plans: Book 2
Supporting water safety management for urban piped water supplies in developing countries

Document 3

Water Safety Plans: Book 3
Risk assessment of contaminant intrusion into water distribution systems

Document 4

Water Safety Plans: Book 4
IRA-WDS software and manual for risk assessment of contaminant intrusion into water distribution systems

CONTENTS

Chapter 1:   IRA-WDS Overview   1

Chapter 2:   Data Preparation   11

List of tables

List of figures

CHAPTER ONE

IRA-WDS: Overview

Manual of Risk Assessment for Contaminant Intrusion into Water Distribution Systems

Chapter-1
IRA-WDS: Overview

Chapter-2
Data Preparation

Chapter-3
Contaminant Ingress Model

Chapter-4
Pipe Condition Assessment Model

Chapter-5
Risk Assessment Model

Chapter 1: IRA-WDS Overview

1.1 System setup

The recommended screen settings for IRA-WDS are 1024 x 768. Lower settings may result in some parts of the input dialogue boxes being partially displayed.

1.1.1 Hardware and software requirements

Hardware and software requirements for IRA-WDS are similar to those of standard PC-based ArcView 3.1 or 3.2. Memory and compatibility requirements for the installation of IRA-WDS are presented in Table 1.1, below.

For three-dimensional visualization of the results from IRA-WDS, ArcView 3D Analyst and Spatial Analyst software need to be installed with ArcView, these having to be obtained separately.

Table 1.1. Hardware and software requirements		
Hardware/Software	**Minimum requirements**	**Preferred requirements**
Processor	Pentium III 1GHz	Pentium IV 2.2GHz or above
Hard disk space	100MB	1GB
Random Access Memory (RAM)	128Mb of RAM plus 256Mb of permanent virtual memory swap space	512Mb of RAM plus 512Mb of permanent virtual memory swap space
Colour monitor	Configured for 16-bit high colours, resolution 1024 x 768	Configured for 32-bit true colours, resolution 1024 x 768
Operating system	Windows 98, 2000, NT	Windows 2000 or Windows XP professional
ArcView	ArcView Version 3.2, 3D Analyst	ArcView 3.2, 3D and Spatial Analyst

Microsoft Excel 2000/XP is recommended for use. Internet Explorer 6.0 or a more recent version is required to view help files.

3

1.1.2 Arc View 3.1/3.2

ArcView is not software in the public domain. It is a desktop Geographic Information System developed by ESRI. With ArcView, one can create intelligent, dynamic maps using data from virtually any source and across most popular computing platforms. ArcView provides the tools to allow the user to work with maps, database tables, charts and graphics all at once. One can also use multimedia links to add pictures, sound and video to the maps generated. ArcView makes it easy to integrate data from overall organization and work with the datageographically. Using ArcView software's powerful visualization tools, one can access records from existing databases and display them on maps. Using Avenue, which is ArcView software's built-in object-oriented scripting language, one can develop custom tools, interfaces and complete applications.

ArcView can be purchased from the ESRI store direct and costs approximately $1,195.00 for the Windows platform and $2,195.00 for the UNIX platform. More information can be obtained from <http://www.esri.com/software/arcview/how-to-buy.html> or by contacting a local ESRI distributor.

ArcView comes with several extensions for carrying out different tasks. Extensions are plug-ins that one can load and unload according to need. 3D Analyst and Spatial Analyst are the most useful extensions in environmental modelling studies. However, these are supplied as optional extensions and one has to procure or purchase them separately. IRA-WDS has been developed using ArcView's built-in macro language, Avenue.

The extensions, 3D Analyst and Spatial Analyst are not necessary for running IRA-WDS software. However, in order to view results in a three-dimensional or perspective view, one must have ArcView's 3D Analyst extension installed. At the same time, if one is to perform spatial analysis of results by buffering, overlaying and so on, one must have ArcView's Spatial Analyst extension installed on the computer.

1.2 Installing the interface

The set-up installs the ArcView interface for IRA-WDS, which has been formatted to create a two separate directory structure on the local hard disk.

First it creates an 'AVIRAWDS' folder on the 'C:\' drive. In this folder, subdirectories named 'Legends' and 'Help' are created. The ArcView Legend files for various themes are copied to the 'C:\AVIRAWDS\Legends' subdirectory. The IRA-WDS html Help files are copied to the 'C:\AVIRAWDS\Help' subdirectory.

The second folder is created in a user-specified path. In this folder, four subdirectories named 'Help', 'Logo', 'Project' and 'Sample Data' are created. The Excel files stating the data requirements for Ingress and Pipe Condition Assessment themes are copied to the 'Help' subdirectory. The Logo files are copied to 'Logo' subdirectory. The IRA-WDS default start-up ArcView Project File 'irawds.apr' is copied to the 'Project' subdirectory. The sample data for analysis of the model is copied to the 'Sample Data' subdirectory.

The IRA-WDS ArcView extension file 'ira-wds.avx' is copied to ArcView's EXT32 folder, which is normally placed in the 'C:\ESRI\AV_GIS30\ARCVIEW\EXT32' path. The dynamic link libraries of the Contamination Ingress Model 'ingress.dll', Pipe Condition Assessment Model 'pca.dll', Risk Assessment Model 'risk.dll' and Analytical Hierarchy Process sub model 'ahp.dll' are copied to ArcView's 'BIN32' folder, which is normally placed in the 'C:\ESRI\AV_GIS30\ARCVIEW\BIN32' path.

To install the interface:

1 Double click on the IRA-WDS Setup.exe

IRASetup

2 'Welcome' screen will appear. Click [Next >]

3 'Information' screen will appear. Click [Next >]

4 'License Agreement' screen will appear. Click ⊙ I agree with the above terms and conditions

and then click [Next >]

5 Choose the installation directory. And then click [Next >]

6 'Confirmation' screen will appear. Click [Start]

The setup will copy 'ira-wds.avx' file to the ArcView extension directory.

The setup will copy 'ahp.dll', 'ingress.dll', 'pca.dll' and 'risk.dll' to '$AVBIN'.

The setup will copy the Sample Data files, Project file and Uninstallation file to the directory chosen by the user.

If the Installation directory is other than 'C:\AVIRAWDS', then set-up will create a folder 'AVIRAWDS' on the C: drive and will copy Legend and Help files into the Legend and Help directories.

7 'End' screen will appear. Click [Next >]

'Clickteam Installation Creator Pro' screen will appear. Click [Exit]

Installation is complete. Shortcut will appear on desktop and

IRA-WDS is ready for use.

The directory structure created by installation of the IRA-WDS interface is displayed below:

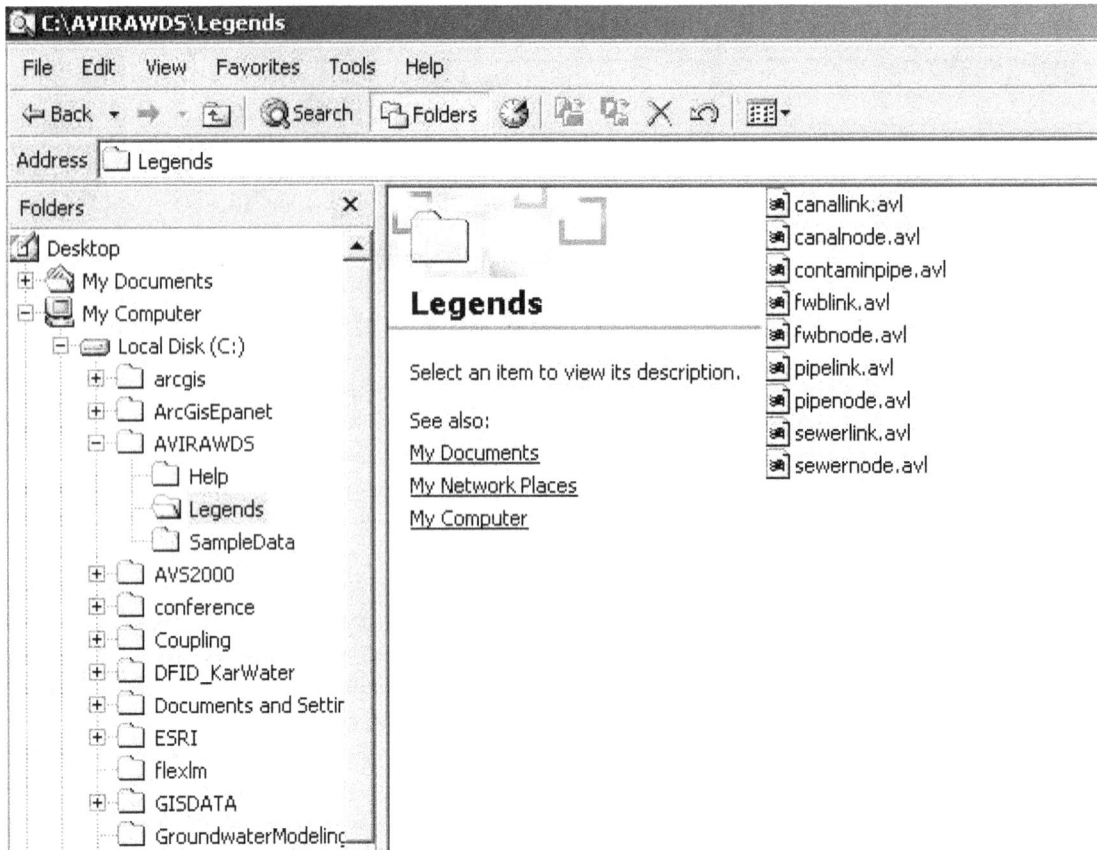

1.3 Uninstalling the interface

The IRA-WDS interface can be uninstalled in number of ways. It is recommended to uninstall the software by running the 'uninstal.exe' from the installation directory. The uninstalling steps are given below.

1   Click   **start**   on desktop.

2   Go to   Programs   ▶

3   Go to   IRA - WDS   ▶

4   Click on the   ✗ Uninstall IRA - WDS

Uninstallation removes IRA-WDS from the programs menu, deletes 'ahp.dll', 'ingress.dll', 'pca.dll', 'risk.dll' and 'IRA-WDS.avx' from ArcView installation paths and removes all legend files, help files, sample data files and 'IRA-WDS.apr' from the respective installation directories.

1.4 Using IRA-WDS

IRA-WDS can be run either by double clicking

or from taskbar as

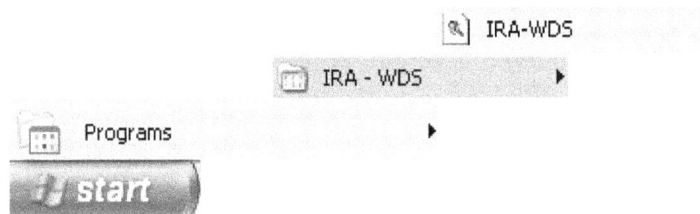

Then following IRA-WDS 'Welcome' screen will appear:

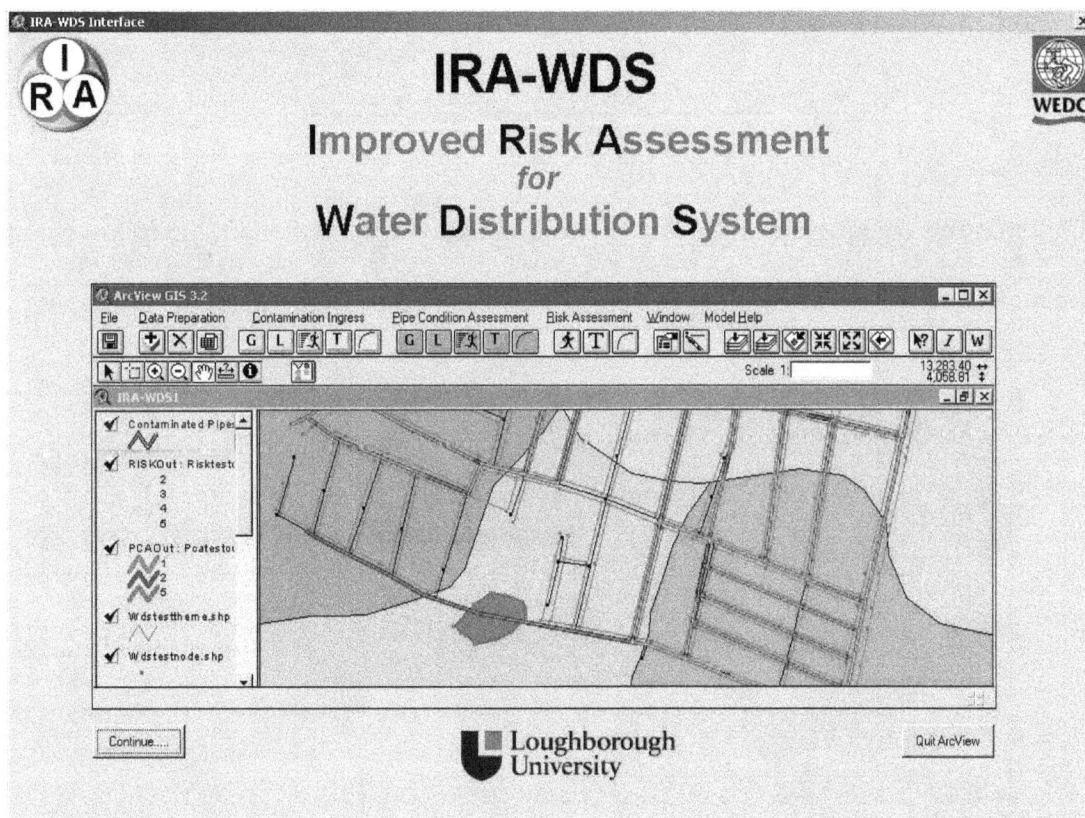

Clicking Quit ArcView will exit IRA-WDS

and clicking Continue..... will take you to following screen:

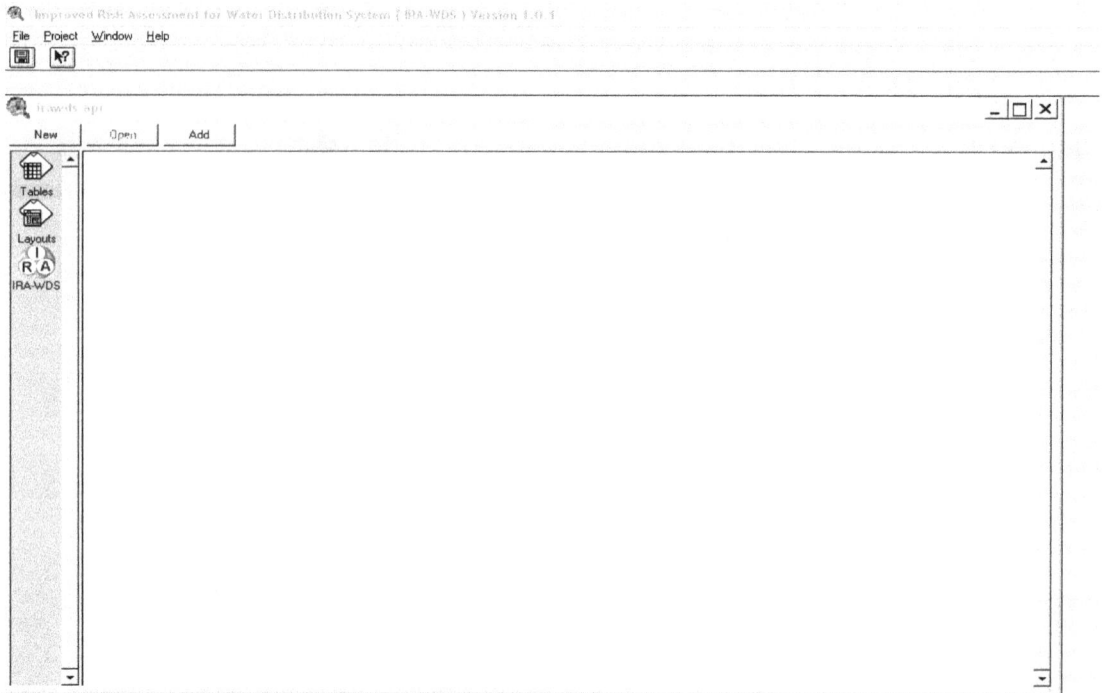

After double clicking on 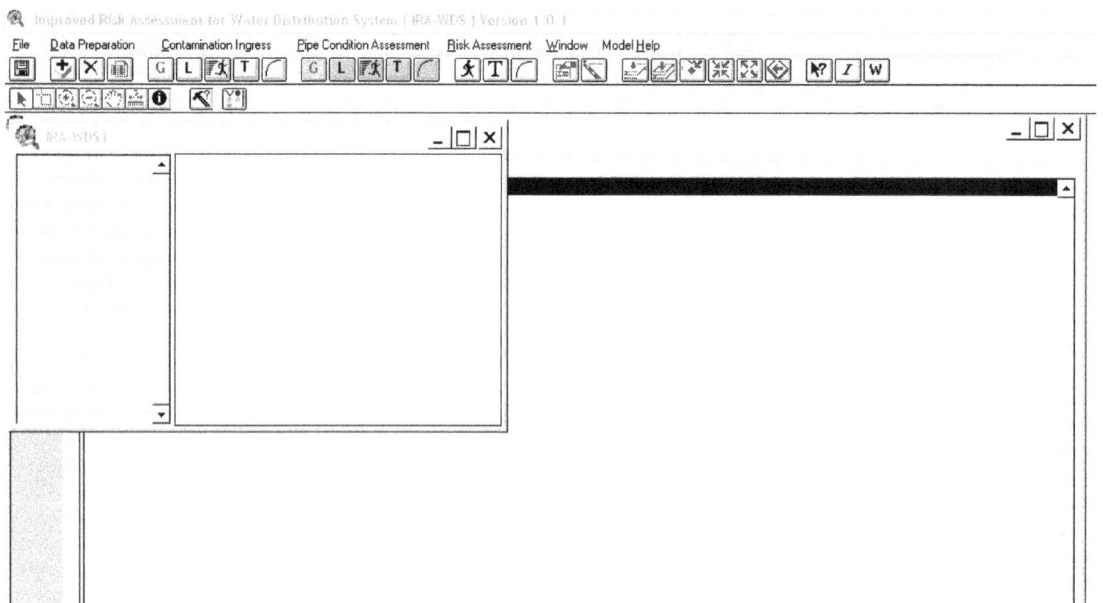 from the menu on the left, the following

main IRA-WDS screen will appear:

IRA-WDS has following seven main menus. One or more of these menus needs to be used in order to obtain results from IRA-WDS.

1   File

2   Data Preparation

3   Contamination Ingress

4   Pipe Condition Assessment

5   Risk Assessment

6   Window

7   Model Help

1.4.1 File menu

After clicking on 'File', the user gains access to following options:

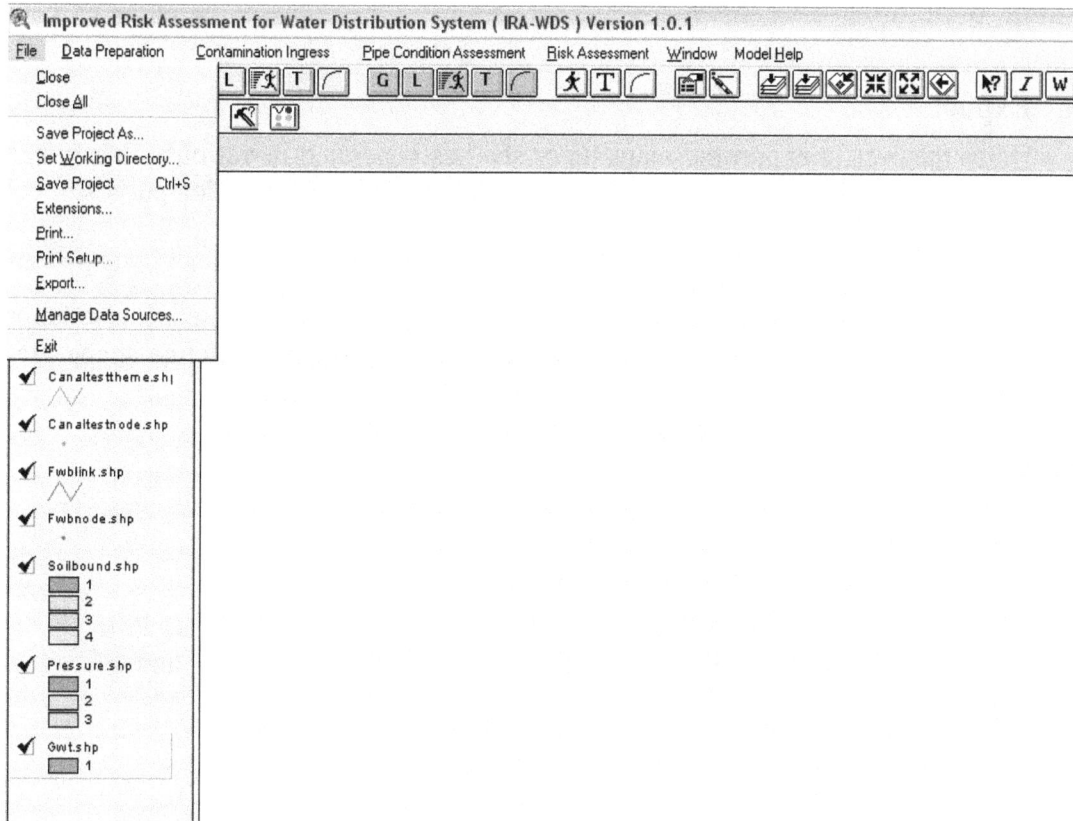

1. **Close and Close All:**

   Helps in closing a single opened document or Graphical User Interface (GUI) or all opened documents or GUIs.

2. **Save Project and Save Project As:**

   Helps in saving the current project or saving it with a different name.

3. **Set Working Directory:**

   Helps in setting the current project work directory so that the user will be prompted to 'Choose/Save/Load' his or her work to or from the directory set at every instance of the file 'Open/Save' dialogue box.

4. **Extensions:**

   Helps the user to load other extensions to the IRA-WDS interface, if required.

5. **Print:**

   Helps the user to set the printer and printing properties, and to print the maps he or she has generated.

6. **Export:**

   Helps the user to export the maps he or she has generated in various other image formats so that he or she can use them for publication or presentation purposes.

7. **Manage data source:**

   Helps the user to manage the shape files data he or she has generated. It also helps the user to perform operations such as copying, renaming and deleting shape files easily.

8. **Exit:**

   Helps the user to exit from the IRA-WDS interface and ArcView.

Note: Details of the menus Data Preparation, Contaminant Ingress, Pipe Condition and Risk Assessment are provided in Chapters 2, 3, 4 and 5, respectively.

CHAPTER TWO

Data Preparation

Manual of Risk Assessment for Contaminant Intrusion into Water Distribution System

Chapter-1
IRA-WDS: Overview

Chapter-2
Data Preparation

Chapter-3
Contaminant Ingress Model

Chapter-4
Pipe Condition Assessment Model

Chapter-5
Risk Assessment Model

Chapter 2: Data Preparation

2.1 Introduction

Data preparation for the IRA-WDS program involves two major steps:

1. The creation of appropriate shape files: these are GIS files that contain the spatial information on all objects considered by the IRA-WDS program; and
2. Input of additional model data: these files contain specific characteristics of the objects generated in the shape files.

2.2 Creating shape files

The first step in using IRA-WDS is to create a series of **shape files** (for ArcView). These shape files contain spatial information on the various objects considered by IRA-WDS. These include: pollution sources, water distribution systems, base maps (that is, infrastructure and contour maps) and environmental maps (for example, soil type, groundwater and so on). The shape files are generated by digitizing maps containing the various objects (pollution sources, water distribution systems, base maps etc.); see Figures 2.1 and 2.2, below. Shape files can be divided into two categories:

- Thematic layers: base maps and environmental maps; and
- Network databases: pollution sources and water distribution systems.

As mentioned above, pollution sources and water distribution pipes are all represented as networks within IRA-WDS. For the purposes of modelling, the geometry of the networks has to be expressed as a network consisting of links and nodes. The links and nodes act as a framework on which all other kinds of relevant information are hung. The shape files so generated contain the following information:

- Nodal shape files: *Node id, x-coord, y-coord* and *Elevation*; and
- Link shape files: *Link id, Start node, End node* and *Length.*

13

The shape files required for IRA-WDS are as follows:

- Sewer node and link shape files;
- Canal node and link shape files;
- Foul surface water body node and link shape files; and
- Water distribution node and link shape files.

Note that in the user's working directory, each shape file generated will have five separate files associated with it with the following extensions: *.shp, *.shr, *.sbx, *.spn and *.dbf. For example, a sewer node shape file will have five associated files.

Among these five files, the most important ones are the '**shp**' and '**dbf**' files:

- The 'shp' files are uploaded through the GIS interface to run the program; and
- The 'dbf' files contain all the attribute data for nodes and links. These files are expanded during the data preparation stage (described in Section 2.3), to include specific characteristics of the nodes and links.

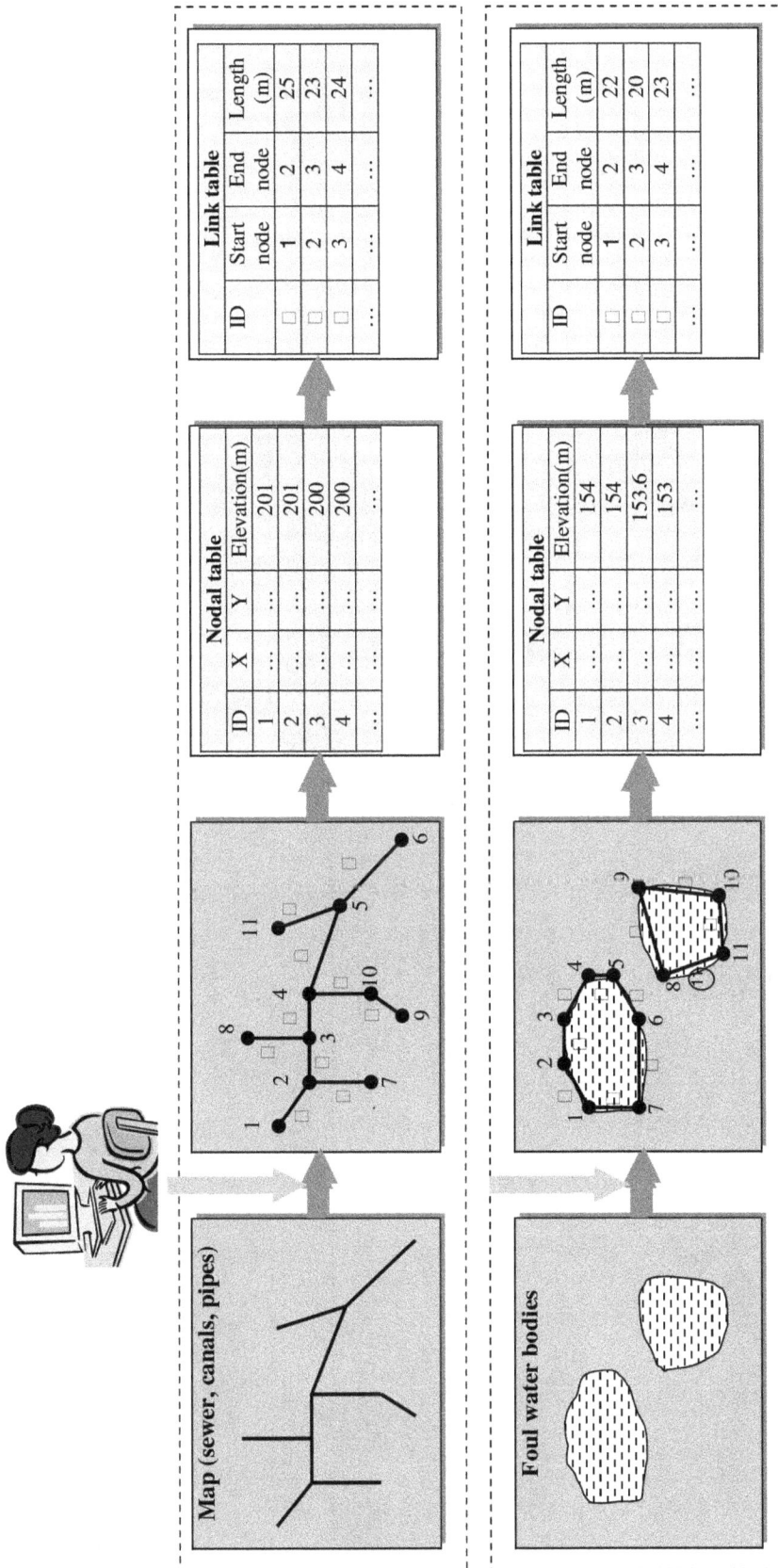

Figure 2.1. Digitization of real-world network

Pressure table

ID	Area	Perimeter	Pressure		
P1	90813	996	High	...	
P2	98712	1523	Medium	...	
P3	94327	1265	Low	...	
...	...	...	...	...	

GWT table

ID	Area	Perimeter	Avg_GWTDep	Avg_GWTFlc	
Z1	2565	2053	14	2	...
Z2	4563	6087	13	2	...
Z3	7856	10652	11	2	...
Z4	6753	11056	9	2	...
...	...	...	...	...	

Soil bound

ID	Area	Perimeter	SAT_K	SAT_MC	
□	65356	1066	29.590	0.430	...
□	67543	1158	14.360	0.410	...
□	72314	1340	4.212	0.410	...
...	...	...	...	...	

Basic pressure map

Groundwater map

Soil map

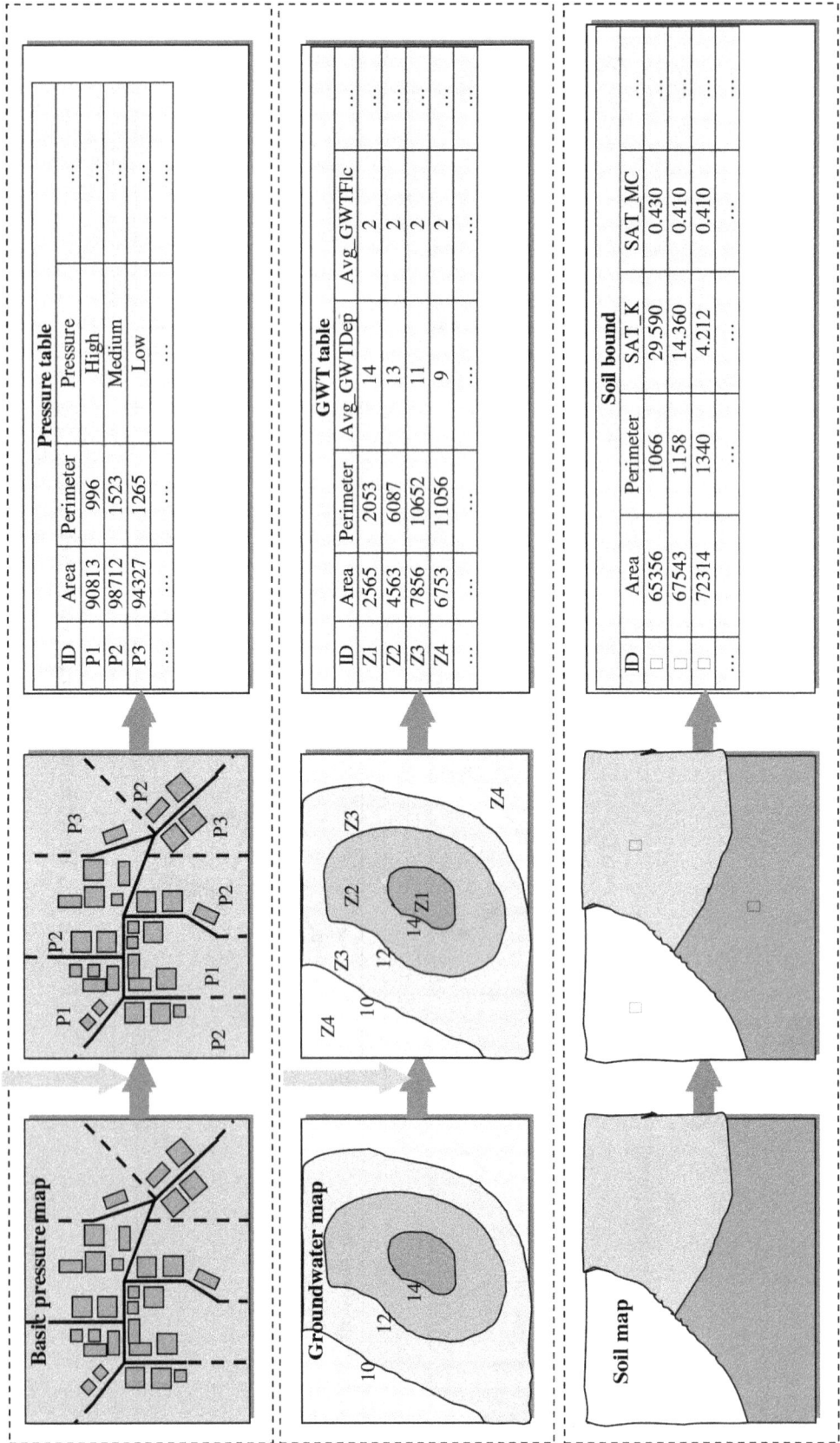

Figure 2.2. Digitization of thematic maps

Output

On completion of this step (creating shape-files) a number of shape files will have been created. These may include:

<u>Thematic Layers</u>

- Base maps:
    - ➤ Infrastructure – *Line and Polygon shape files*
    - ➤ Contour – *Line shape files*

- Environmental maps:
    - ➤ Soil – *Polygon shape files*
    - ➤ Groundwater – *Polygon shape files*
    - ➤ Pressure – *Polygon shape files*

<u>Network databases</u>

- Sewer – *Node and Link shape files*
- Canal – *Node and Link shape files*
- Foul water body – *Node and Link shape files*
- Water distribution – *Node and Link shape files*

2.3 Input of additional model data

2.3.1 Enclosed Excel spreadsheet (DataInput.xls)

In this section, details of how to add additional node and link data to the shape files are presented. To assist in this, an Excel file has been included with IRA-WDS (DataInput.xls) that contains a template. Figure 2.3, below, shows example worksheets from the Excel file.

The first thing for the user to do is to copy this Excel file into his or her working directory and rename it as appropriate (for example, the project name). The Excel spread sheet contains several worksheets to assist with data entry.

The first worksheet labelled 'General Description' gives an overview of all the other worksheets and provides information on data requirements for those other worksheets (see Figure 2.3). Hyperlinks are provided in this worksheet to help navigate between the other worksheets.

In addition to the General Description worksheet, there are 12 other worksheets (see the tabs at the bottom of the worksheet shown in Figure 2.3). In each of these 12 worksheets, attribute data for the various objects are added by the user. On completion of these worksheets, the data contained in them are then transferred to the objects' respective shape files (details of how this is done is given in Section 2.4).

Note that this Excel spreadsheet has several columns in each worksheet, where the data have already been generated and stored in the shape files (in the file with extension dbf). These data mainly relate to the spatial location of the objects, but also include information related to elevation and lengths of links.

Therefore the authors suggest that the data from the shape files (dbf) are copied and pasted into the appropriate worksheet of the Excel file.

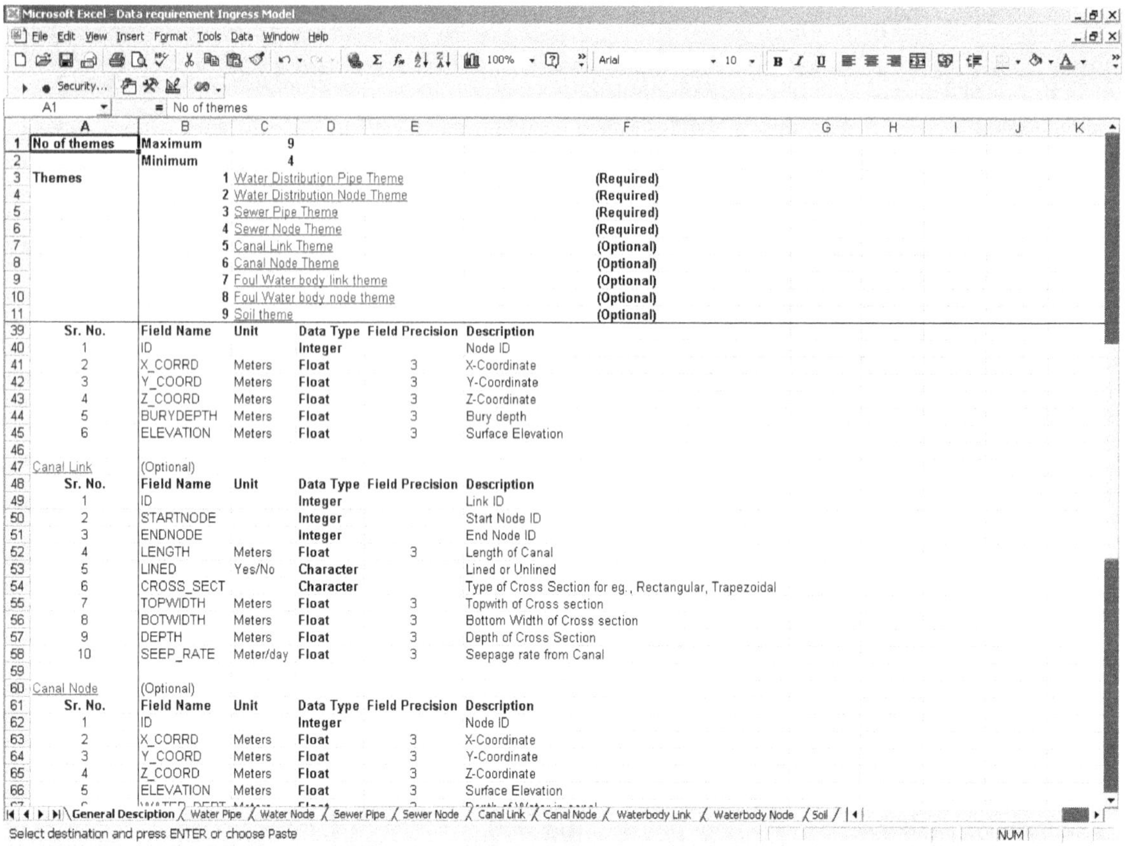

	A	B	C	D	E	F
1	No of themes	Maximum		9		
2		Minimum		4		
3	Themes		1	Water Distribution Pipe Theme		(Required)
4			2	Water Distribution Node Theme		(Required)
5			3	Sewer Pipe Theme		(Required)
6			4	Sewer Node Theme		(Required)
7			5	Canal Link Theme		(Optional)
8			6	Canal Node Theme		(Optional)
9			7	Foul Water body link theme		(Optional)
10			8	Foul Water body node theme		(Optional)
11			9	Soil theme		(Optional)
39	Sr. No.	Field Name	Unit	Data Type	Field Precision	Description
40	1	ID		Integer		Node ID
41	2	X_CORRD	Meters	Float	3	X-Coordinate
42	3	Y_COORD	Meters	Float	3	Y-Coordinate
43	4	Z_COORD	Meters	Float	3	Z-Coordinate
44	5	BURYDEPTH	Meters	Float	3	Bury depth
45	6	ELEVATION	Meters	Float	3	Surface Elevation
46						
47	Canal Link	(Optional)				
48	Sr. No.	Field Name	Unit	Data Type	Field Precision	Description
49	1	ID		Integer		Link ID
50	2	STARTNODE		Integer		Start Node ID
51	3	ENDNODE		Integer		End Node ID
52	4	LENGTH	Meters	Float	3	Length of Canal
53	5	LINED	Yes/No	Character		Lined or Unlined
54	6	CROSS_SECT		Character		Type of Cross Section for eg., Rectangular, Trapezoidal
55	7	TOPWIDTH	Meters	Float	3	Topwith of Cross section
56	8	BOTWIDTH	Meters	Float	3	Bottom Width of Cross section
57	9	DEPTH	Meters	Float	3	Depth of Cross Section
58	10	SEEP_RATE	Meter/day	Float	3	Seepage rate from Canal
59						
60	Canal Node	(Optional)				
61	Sr. No.	Field Name	Unit	Data Type	Field Precision	Description
62	1	ID		Integer		Node ID
63	2	X_CORRD	Meters	Float	3	X-Coordinate
64	3	Y_COORD	Meters	Float	3	Y-Coordinate
65	4	Z_COORD	Meters	Float	3	Z-Coordinate
66	5	ELEVATION	Meters	Float	3	Surface Elevation

Figure 2.3. Enclosed Excel file DataInput.xls

2.3.2 Contaminant Ingress Model

The data required for the Contaminant Ingress Model are as follows:

- Pollutant sources;
- Water distribution pipes; and
- Environmental data (soil type and so on).

2.3.2.1 Pollutant sources

IRA-WDS considers the following pollutant sources: sewers/drains, canals and ponds/ditches. As described earlier, the spatial information about the pollution sources is contained in the generated shape files. This section provides details on how additional attribute data are added.

Figure 2.4, below, shows the relevant worksheet for pollutant sources from the enclosed Excel file.

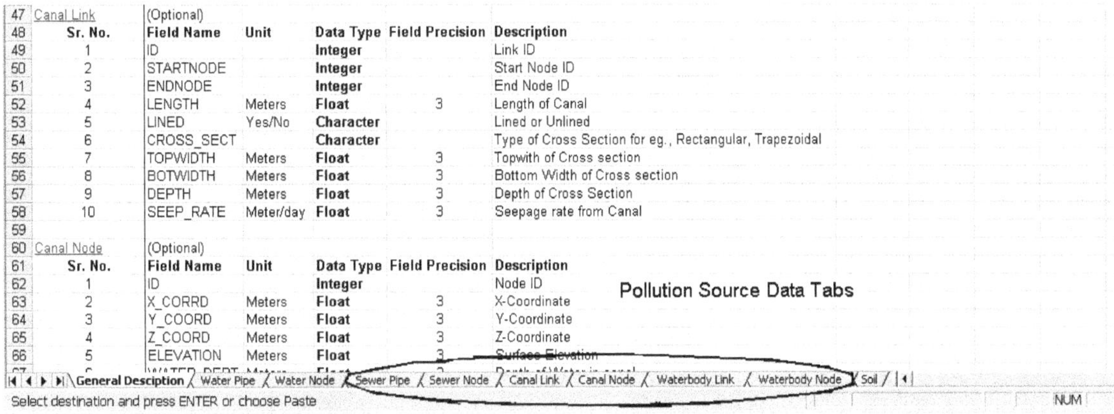

47	Canal Link	(Optional)				
48	**Sr. No.**	**Field Name**	**Unit**	**Data Type**	**Field Precision**	**Description**
49	1	ID		**Integer**		Link ID
50	2	STARTNODE		**Integer**		Start Node ID
51	3	ENDNODE		**Integer**		End Node ID
52	4	LENGTH	Meters	**Float**	3	Length of Canal
53	5	LINED	Yes/No	**Character**		Lined or Unlined
54	6	CROSS_SECT		**Character**		Type of Cross Section for eg., Rectangular, Trapezoidal
55	7	TOPWIDTH	Meters	**Float**	3	Topwith of Cross section
56	8	BOTWIDTH	Meters	**Float**	3	Bottom Width of Cross section
57	9	DEPTH	Meters	**Float**	3	Depth of Cross Section
58	10	SEEP_RATE	Meter/day	**Float**	3	Seepage rate from Canal
59						
60	Canal Node	(Optional)				
61	**Sr. No.**	**Field Name**	**Unit**	**Data Type**	**Field Precision**	**Description**
62	1	ID		**Integer**		Node ID
63	2	X_CORRD	Meters	**Float**	3	X-Coordinate
64	3	Y_COORD	Meters	**Float**	3	Y-Coordinate
65	4	Z_COORD	Meters	**Float**	3	Z-Coordinate
66	5	ELEVATION	Meters	**Float**	3	Surface Elevation

Figure 2.4. Worksheet for pollutant sources

At this stage:

- The Excel spreadsheet should have been saved in the user's working directory; and
- The shaded columns shown in Figures 2.5 and Figure 2.6 should be filled from the data in the dbf shape files (see Section 2.4).

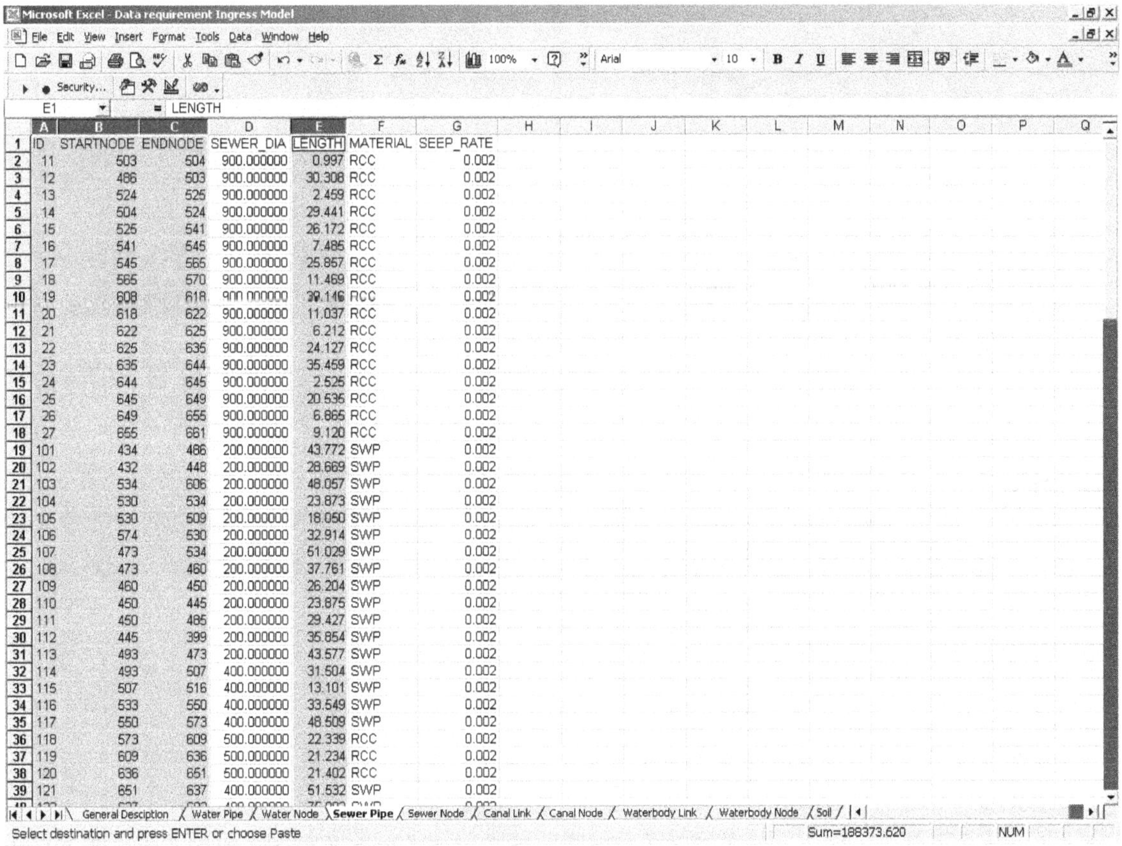

	ID	STARTNODE	ENDNODE	SEWER_DIA	LENGTH	MATERIAL	SEEP_RATE
2	11	503	504	900.000000	0.997	RCC	0.002
3	12	486	503	900.000000	30.308	RCC	0.002
4	13	524	525	900.000000	2.459	RCC	0.002
5	14	504	524	900.000000	29.441	RCC	0.002
6	15	525	541	900.000000	26.172	RCC	0.002
7	16	541	545	900.000000	7.485	RCC	0.002
8	17	545	565	900.000000	25.857	RCC	0.002
9	18	565	570	900.000000	11.469	RCC	0.002
10	19	608	618	900.000000	39.146	RCC	0.002
11	20	618	622	900.000000	11.037	RCC	0.002
12	21	622	625	900.000000	6.212	RCC	0.002
13	22	625	635	900.000000	24.127	RCC	0.002
14	23	635	644	900.000000	35.459	RCC	0.002
15	24	644	645	900.000000	2.525	RCC	0.002
16	25	645	649	900.000000	20.535	RCC	0.002
17	26	649	655	900.000000	6.865	RCC	0.002
18	27	655	661	900.000000	9.120	RCC	0.002
19	101	434	486	200.000000	43.772	SWP	0.002
20	102	432	448	200.000000	28.669	SWP	0.002
21	103	534	606	200.000000	48.057	SWP	0.002
22	104	530	534	200.000000	23.873	SWP	0.002
23	105	530	509	200.000000	18.050	SWP	0.002
24	106	574	530	200.000000	32.914	SWP	0.002
25	107	473	534	200.000000	51.029	SWP	0.002
26	108	473	460	200.000000	37.761	SWP	0.002
27	109	460	450	200.000000	26.204	SWP	0.002
28	110	450	445	200.000000	23.875	SWP	0.002
29	111	450	485	200.000000	29.427	SWP	0.002
30	112	445	399	200.000000	35.854	SWP	0.002
31	113	493	473	200.000000	43.577	SWP	0.002
32	114	493	507	400.000000	31.504	SWP	0.002
33	115	507	516	400.000000	13.101	SWP	0.002
34	116	533	550	400.000000	33.549	SWP	0.002
35	117	550	573	400.000000	48.509	SWP	0.002
36	118	573	609	500.000000	22.339	RCC	0.002
37	119	609	636	500.000000	21.234	RCC	0.002
38	120	636	651	500.000000	21.402	RCC	0.002
39	121	651	637	400.000000	51.532	SWP	0.002

Figure 2.5. Link data entry for sewer

The next stage is for the user to complete the remaining fields on the worksheets (that is, the unshaded columns of the tables in Figures 2.5 and 2.6). Tables 2.1 and 2.2, below, give details of the additional attributes required for link data and node data respectively for the sewer.

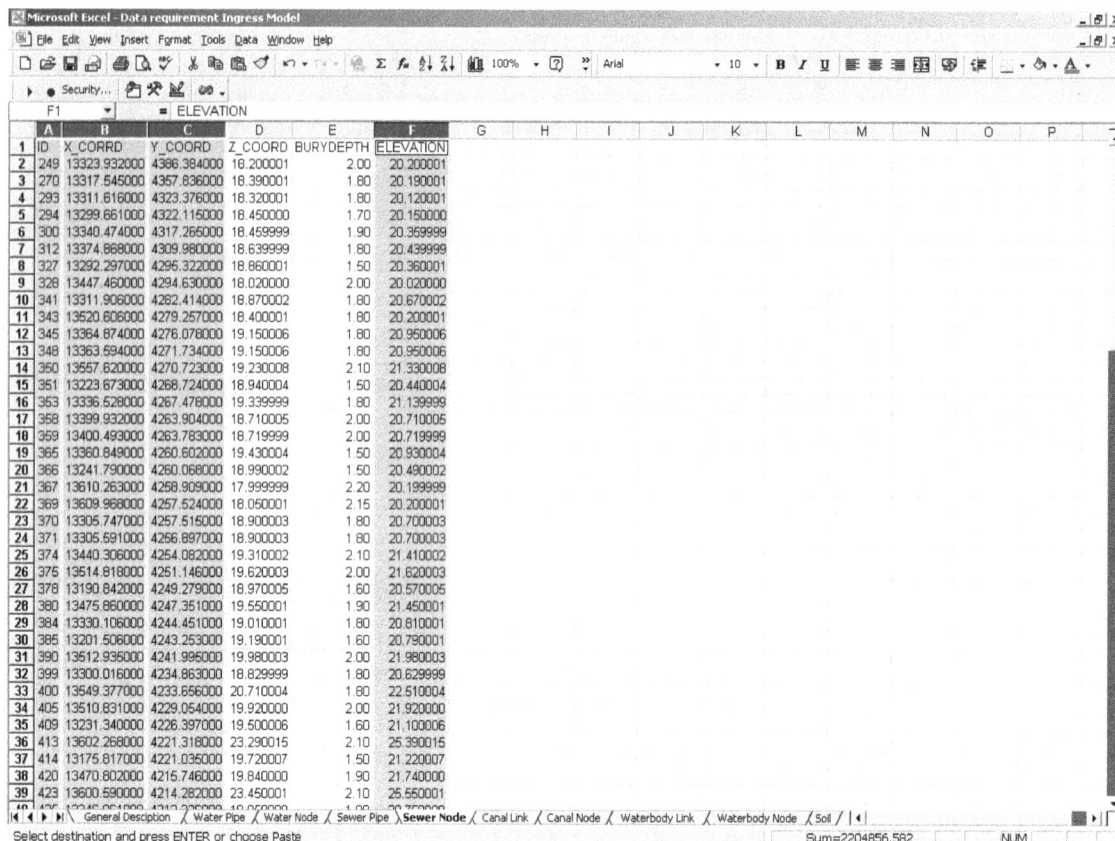

Figure 2.6. Node data entry for sewer

Table 2.1. Sewer link data for Contaminant Ingress Model		
Field name	**Unit**	**Description**
SEWER_DIA	*mm*	Sewer diameter
SEEP_RATE	*Metre/day*	Seepage rate from sewer pipe

Table 2.2. Sewer node data for Contaminant Ingress Model		
Field name	**Unit**	**Description**
BURYDEPTH	*Metres*	Buried depth of node

2.3.2.2 Water distribution system

In addition to pollutant sources, IRA-WDS requires additional attribute data for the water distribution system. As described earlier, the spatial information about the water distribution system (WDS) is contained in the shape files generated earlier. In this section, details are given on how additional attribute data are added.

Figure 2.7, below, shows the relevant worksheet from the enclosed Excel file for the water distribution system. At this stage, the shaded columns shown in Figure 2.7 should have been filled from the data in the dbf shape files (see Section 2.4).

The next stage is for the user to complete the remaining fields on the worksheets (the unshaded columns of the table in Figure 2.7). For details, see Table 2.3.

Table 2.3. WDS node data for Contaminant Ingress Model		
Field name	**Unit**	**Description**
BURYDEPTH	*Metres*	Bury depth
Z- Coordinate	*Metres*	Surface elevation

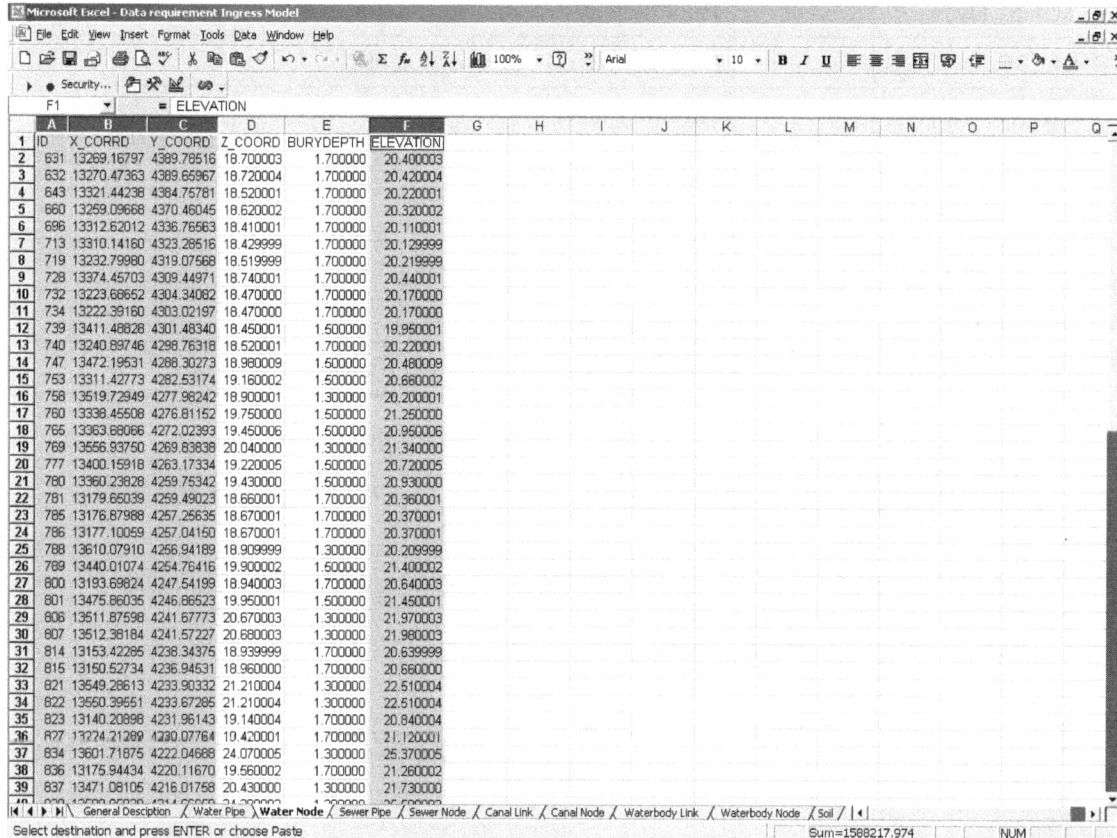

Figure 2.7. Node data entry for water distribution system

2.3.2.3 Environmental factors

In addition to the pollutant sources and water distribution system, IRA-WDS requires information on soil characteristics. Shape files have already been constructed for soil data, groundwater and pressure zones. In this section, details on are given how additional attribute data are added.

Figure 2.8, below, shows the relevant worksheet from the enclosed Excel file for soil characteristics. At this stage, the shaded columns shown in Figure 2.8 should have already been filled from the data in the dbf shape files (see Section 2.4).

The next stage is for the user to complete the remaining fields on the worksheets (the unshaded columns of the table in Figure 2.8). For details, see Table 2.4.

Table 2.4. Soil data for Contaminant Ingress Model		
Field name	**Unit**	**Description**
SAT_K	*cm/hr*	Saturated hydraulic conductivity
SAT_MC		Saturated moisture content
INI_MC		Initial moisture content
BULK_DEN	*gm/cm³*	Bulk density
KOC		Soil organic carbon coefficient
AIR_ENTRY	*cm*	Air entry head
PORESIZE		Pore size index
DIFF_COEFF	*cm²/day*	Diffusion coefficient
SOIL_FOC		Soil fraction of organic content
LIQ_DECAY	*per hr*	Liquid phase decay
CHAR_COEFF		Soil characteristic curve coefficient

Figure 2.8. Soil data entry

2.3.3 Pipe Condition Assessment Model

Data requirements for the Pipe Condition Assessment Model are related to the factors that affect the condition of the pipe. A description of these various factors and how they are represented in the model can be found in Chapter 3, below.

It should be noted that this model requires some data in the form of fuzzy (qualitative) numbers (such as link joint type, surface type, traffic load and so on) and others as crisp (quantitative) numbers (such as link material, diameter, length and so on). Therefore the data in the form of fuzzy numbers will require the user to input fuzzy membership functions. Table 3.1 in Chapter 3 of Book 3 shows which data is fuzzy and which is crisp.

Figure 2.9, below, shows the relevant worksheet from the enclosed Excel file for the Pipe Condition Assessment Model. At this stage, the shaded columns shown in Figure 2.9 should have already been filled from the data in the dbf shape files (see Section 2.4) and during data preparation for the Contaminant Ingress Model. The next stage is for the user to complete the remaining fields on the worksheets (the unshaded columns in Figure 2.9 and Table 2.5).

Table 2.5. WDS link data for Pipe Condition Assessment Model		
Field name	**Unit**	**Description**
STRJOINT		Joint method at start node
ENDJOINT		Joint method at end node
MATERIAL		Material type
TRAFFIC		Traffic load
SURFACE		Surface type
INTPROT		Internal protection
EXTPROT		External protection
BEDCOND		Bedding condition
WORKMANS		Workmanship
DIAMETER	*mm*	Diameter of pipe
INSTYEAR	*yyyy*	Installation year
LENGTH	*Metres*	Length of pipe
STRDEPTH	*Metres*	Start node bury depth
ENDDEPTH	*Metres*	End node bury depth
NOCONNEC		No. of pipes joined with diameter less than minimum considered
BREAKAGE	*Per year*	No. of breaks per year
LEAKAGE	*lps*	Leakage rate
VALVES		No. of valves
DURATION	*Hrs/day*	Duration of water supply per day
NOOPER	*Per day*	No. of times water supplied per day

23

PIPEID	STARTNODE	ENDNODE	STRJOINT	ENDJOINT	MATERIAL	TRAFFIC	SURFACE	INTPROT	EXTPROT	BEDCOND	WORKMANS	DIAMETER	INSTYEAR	LENGTH	STRDEPTH
689	631	632	Very Good	Very Good	AC	Normal	Very Hard	Medium	Bad	Very Bad	Very Good	500	1955	1.312	1.700
703	632	643	Bad	Bad	AC	Normal	Grassed	Medium	Very Good	Very Good	Bad	500	1955	51.204	1.700
722	660	631	Bad	Bad	RCC	Normal	Grassed	Medium	Very Good	Good	Bad	500	1955	21.792	1.700
762	643	696	Medium	Medium	AC	Normal	Grassed	Medium	Very Good	Good	Medium	400	1955	48.796	1.700
781	696	713	Medium	Medium	AC	Normal	Grassed	Medium	Very Good	Good	Medium	400	1955	13.706	1.700
786	719	660	Medium	Medium	RCC	Normal	Grassed	Medium	Very Good	Bad	Medium	500	1955	57.723	1.700
796	713	728	Medium	Medium	AC	Normal	Grassed	Medium	Very Good	Good	Medium	400	1955	65.787	1.700
800	732	719	Medium	Medium	RCC	Quite	Grassed	Medium	Very Good	Bad	Medium	500	1955	17.325	1.700
803	734	732	Medium	Medium	RCC	Quite	Grassed	Medium	Very Good	Bad	Medium	500	1955	1.848	1.700
808	728	739	Medium	Medium	AC	Normal	Very Hard	Medium	Bad	Good	Good	400	1970	37.878	1.500
809	740	734	Medium	Medium	RCC	Quite	Grassed	Medium	Very Good	Bad	Medium	500	1955	18.990	1.700
818	739	747	Medium	Medium	AC	Normal	Very Hard	Medium	Bad	Good	Good	400	1970	62.121	1.500
824	753	740	Medium	Medium	RCC	Quite	Grassed	Medium	Very Good	Bad	Medium	200	1955	72.374	1.700
830	747	758	Medium	Medium	AC	Normal	Very Hard	Medium	Bad	Good	Very Good	400	1970	48.642	1.300
831	760	753	Medium	Medium	RCC	Quite	Very Hard	Medium	Bad	Bad	Medium	200	1955	27.626	1.500
836	765	728	Medium	Medium	AC	Normal	Very Hard	Medium	Bad	Good	Medium	400	1985	38.946	1.500
837	765	760	Medium	Medium	RCC	Quite	Very Hard	Medium	Bad	Bad	Medium	200	1985	25.876	1.500
842	758	769	Medium	Medium	AC	Normal	Very Hard	Medium	Bad	Good	Very Good	400	1970	38.089	1.300
852	777	765	Medium	Medium	RCC	Quite	Very Hard	Medium	Bad	Bad	Medium	200	1970	37.537	1.500
855	780	765	Medium	Medium	AC	Quite	Very Hard	Medium	Bad	Bad	Medium	200	1985	12.744	1.500
856	781	734	Medium	Medium	U1	Very Quite	Grassed	Bad	Very Good	Bad	Medium	500	1955	61.007	1.700
861	785	781	Medium	Medium	U1	Very Quite	Grassed	Bad	Very Good	Bad	Medium	200	1985	3.559	1.700
862	786	785	Medium	Medium	U1	Very Quite	Grassed	Bad	Very Good	Bad	Medium	200	1985	0.308	1.700
865	769	788	Bad	Bad	AC	Quite	Very Hard	Medium	Bad	Good	Very Good	400	1970	54.684	1.300
866	789	777	Medium	Medium	RCC	Quite	Very Hard	Medium	Bad	Bad	Good	200	1970	40.729	1.500
879	800	786	Bad	Bad	U1	Very Quite	Grassed	Bad	Very Good	Bad	Medium	200	1985	19.124	1.700
880	789	801	Medium	Medium	RCC	Quite	Very Hard	Medium	Bad	Bad	Good	200	1970	36.710	1.500
883	801	806	Medium	Medium	RCC	Quite	Very Hard	Medium	Bad	Bad	Very Good	200	1970	36.367	1.300
884	807	758	Medium	Medium	RCC	Normal	Very Hard	Medium	Bad	Good	Very Good	400	1970	37.144	1.300
885	806	807	Medium	Medium	RCC	Quite	Very Hard	Medium	Bad	Bad	Very Good	200	1970	0.517	1.300
892	814	785	Bad	Bad	U1	Very Quite	Grassed	Bad	Very Good	Bad	Medium	200	1985	30.132	1.700
893	815	814	Bad	Bad	U1	Very Quite	Grassed	Bad	Very Good	Bad	Medium	200	1985	3.216	1.700
898	807	821	Medium	Medium	RCC	Quite	Very Hard	Medium	Bad	Bad	Very Good	200	1970	37.693	1.300
899	821	822	Medium	Medium	RCC	Quite	Very Hard	Medium	Bad	Bad	Very Good	200	1970	1.133	1.300
900	823	815	Bad	Bad	U1	Very Quite	Grassed	Bad	Very Good	Bad	Medium	200	1985	11.459	1.700
905	827	800	Bad	Bad	U1	Very Quite	Grassed	Bad	Very Good	Bad	Medium	200	1985	35.159	1.700
914	834	788	Bad	Bad	AC	Quite	Very Hard	Medium	Bad	Good	Very Good	400	1970	35.883	1.300
916	822	834	Bad	Bad	RCC	Quite	Very Hard	Medium	Bad	Bad	Very Good	200	1970	52.624	1.300

Figure 2.9. Water distribution pipe condition assessment data

2.4 Creating a dbf

At this stage, all data for the model have been completed and entered into the Excel spreadsheet provided. This Excel file should have been stored in the working directory for the project.

The next step is for the user to link the data in the Excel spreadsheet with the relevant shape files. In order to achieve this, each worksheet from the Excel spreadsheet must be saved as a dbf file with a filename identical to the relevant shape file.

For example, to create the link data shape file for a water distribution system:
1. If the name of the shape file is 'waterpipe.shp'
2. In the Excel spreadsheet select the 'WDSlink' worksheet
3. While this worksheet is active, do the following:
   - File – Save As: 'waterpipe.dbf' (this name is the same as the shape file)
   - Make sure the file is saved to the working directory (that contains the shape files)
   - Note: the original 'waterpipe.dbf' file will be overwritten with the new dbf file. Therefore, make sure all the information in the original dbf file has been copied to the new one.

2.5 Add shape files to GIS

The next step is for the user to add the necessary shape files to IRA-WDS, so that the data can be viewed and used by the three models (the Contamination Ingress Model, Pipe Condition Assessment Model and Risk Assessment Model). This can be done by clicking on the Tool icon ⊞ which is just below the 'Data Preparation' menu or by clicking on the 'Data Preparation' menu and then clicking on the submenu 'Add Shape Files to IRA-WDS View', as shown in the screen below:

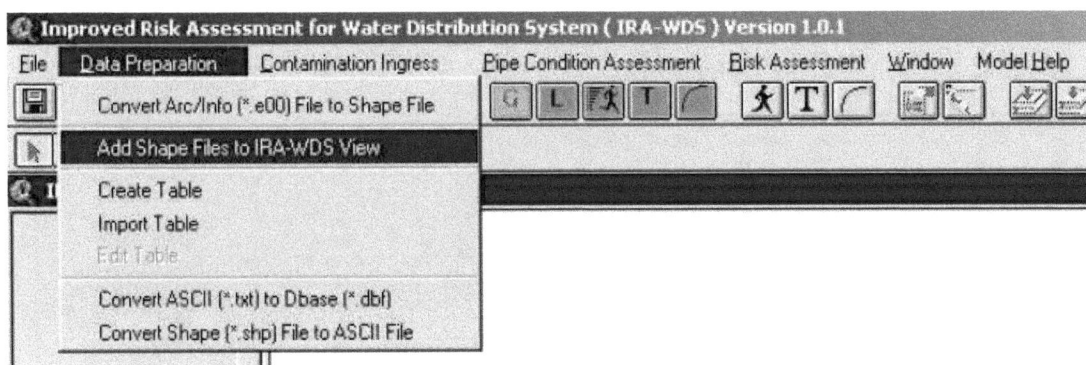

This opens the 'Add Theme' form, as shown below:

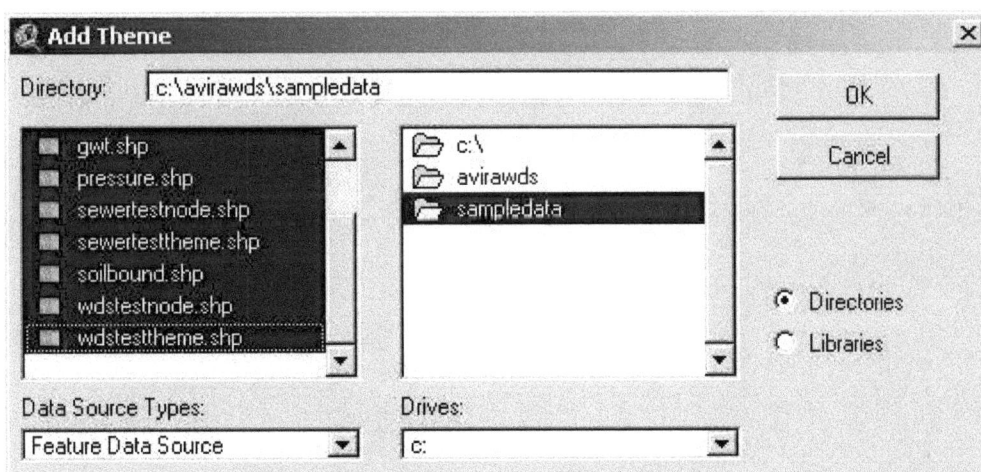

After the user selects the shape files to be added to the IRA-WDS View, he/she can click on the 'OK' button, which will load the shape files to the IRA-WDS View, and corresponding dbf files in the Table GUI of the ArcView.

CHAPTER THREE

Contaminant Ingress Model

Manual of Risk Assessment for Contaminant Intrusion into Water Distribution Systems

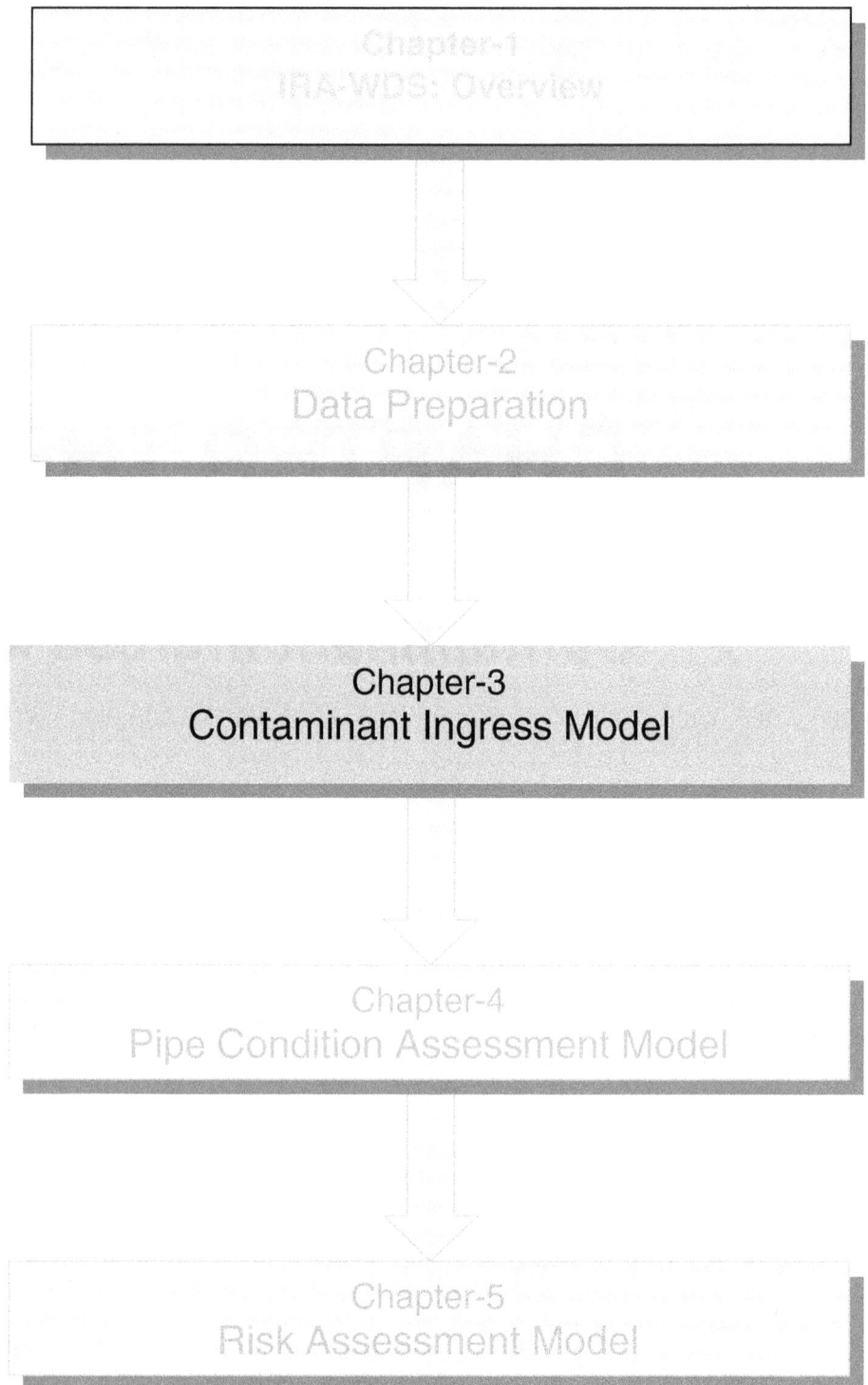

Chapter-1
IRA-WDS: Overview

Chapter-2
Data Preparation

Chapter-3
Contaminant Ingress Model

Chapter-4
Pipe Condition Assessment Model

Chapter-5
Risk Assessment Model

Chapter 3: Contaminant Ingress Model

3.1 Introduction

The 'Contaminant Ingress' menu contains several submenus. This chapter describes the use of these submenus and associated commands to run the Contaminant Ingress Model. Figure 3.1, below, shows the steps involved in executing this component of the software.

The following steps need to be performed to run the Contaminant Ingress Model:

- Adding the data (if not already done so)
- Rearranging the data (optional)
- Generating an input file
- Viewing Ingress input file (optional)
- Loading input file
- Running model
- Displaying output (optional)

The example files given in Table 3.1 are used for illustration purposes to describe the use of the Contaminant Ingress Model with the help of IRA-WDS.

Table 3.1. Example input files	
Themes	**Filenames**
Water distribution	wdstesttheme.shp
	wdstestnode.shp
Sewer	sewertesttheme.shp
	sewertestnode.shp
Canal	canaltesttheme.shp
	canaltestnode.shp
Foul water body	fwblink.shp
	fwbnode.shp
Soil type	soilbound.shp

```
┌─────────────────────────────────────────┐
│ ┌─────────────────────────────────────┐ │
│ │  Contaminant Ingress                │ │
│ │                                     │ │
│ │               ▼                     │ │
│ │  ┌───────────────────────────────┐  │ │
│ │  │  Prepare ingress input database│  │ │
│ │  └───────────────────────────────┘  │ │
│ │               ▼                     │ │
│ │  ┌───────────────────────────────┐  │ │
│ │  │  Generate Contaminant Ingress │  │ │
│ │  │         input files           │  │ │
│ │  └───────────────────────────────┘  │ │
│ │               ▼                     │ │
│ │  ┌───────────────────────────────┐  │ │
│ │  │  View Contaminant Ingress     │  │ │
│ │  │         input files           │  │ │
│ │  └───────────────────────────────┘  │ │
│ │               ▼                     │ │
│ │  ┌───────────────────────────────┐  │ │
│ │  │  Load Contaminant Ingress     │  │ │
│ │  │         input files           │  │ │
│ │  └───────────────────────────────┘  │ │
│ │               ▼                     │ │
│ │  ┌───────────────────────────────┐  │ │
│ │  │  Run Contaminant Ingress      │  │ │
│ │  │         Model                 │  │ │
│ │  └───────────────────────────────┘  │ │
│ │               ▼                     │ │
│ │  ┌───────────────────────────────┐  │ │
│ │  │  Display Contaminant Ingress  │  │ │
│ │  │  output in table/shape format │  │ │
│ │  └───────────────────────────────┘  │ │
│ └─────────────────────────────────────┘ │
└─────────────────────────────────────────┘
```

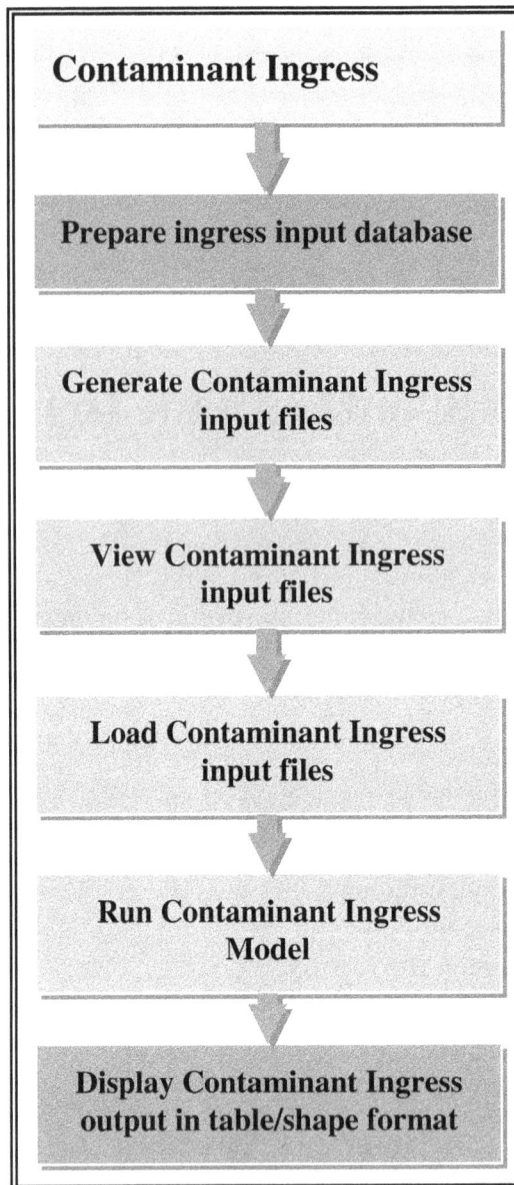

Figure 3.1. Overview of Contaminant Ingress Model of IRA-WDS

3.2 Shape files

3.2.1 Adding shape files

Adding shape files can be done by clicking on the Tool icon ⊞ which is just below the 'Data Preparation' menu or by clicking on the 'Data Preparation' menu and then clicking on the submenu 'Add Shape Files to IRA-WDS View', as shown in the screen below:

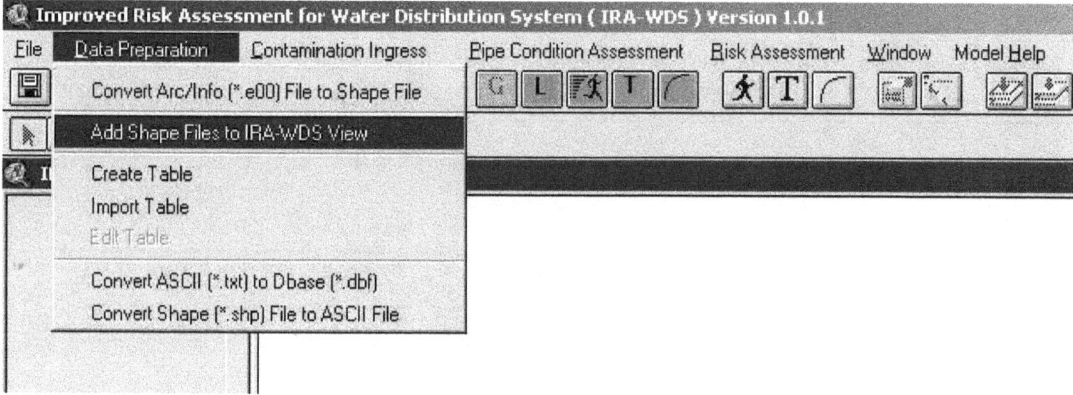

This opens the Add Theme form, as shown below, and the user is then required to select the desired files. At this stage, these files are those relating to: water distribution link and node; sewer pipe link and node; canal link and node; foul water bodies link and node; and soil polygon map.

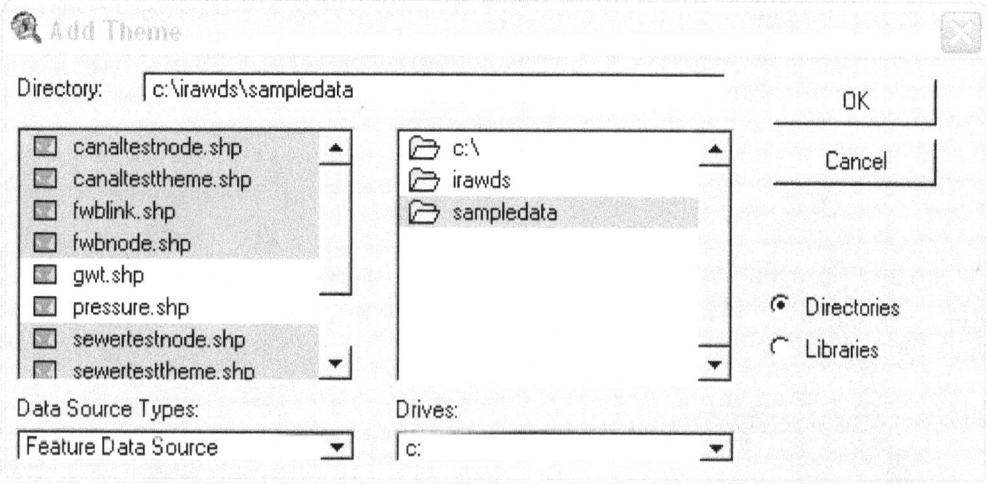

3.2.2 Rearranging shape files

Once the data are added, these can be rearranged for viewing purposes. This can be done by selecting (✔) and/or omitting (⬜) different themes (on the left hand side) and changing the preference order of different themes by dragging them above or below the other themes. For example, the view with only line and node themes is as below:

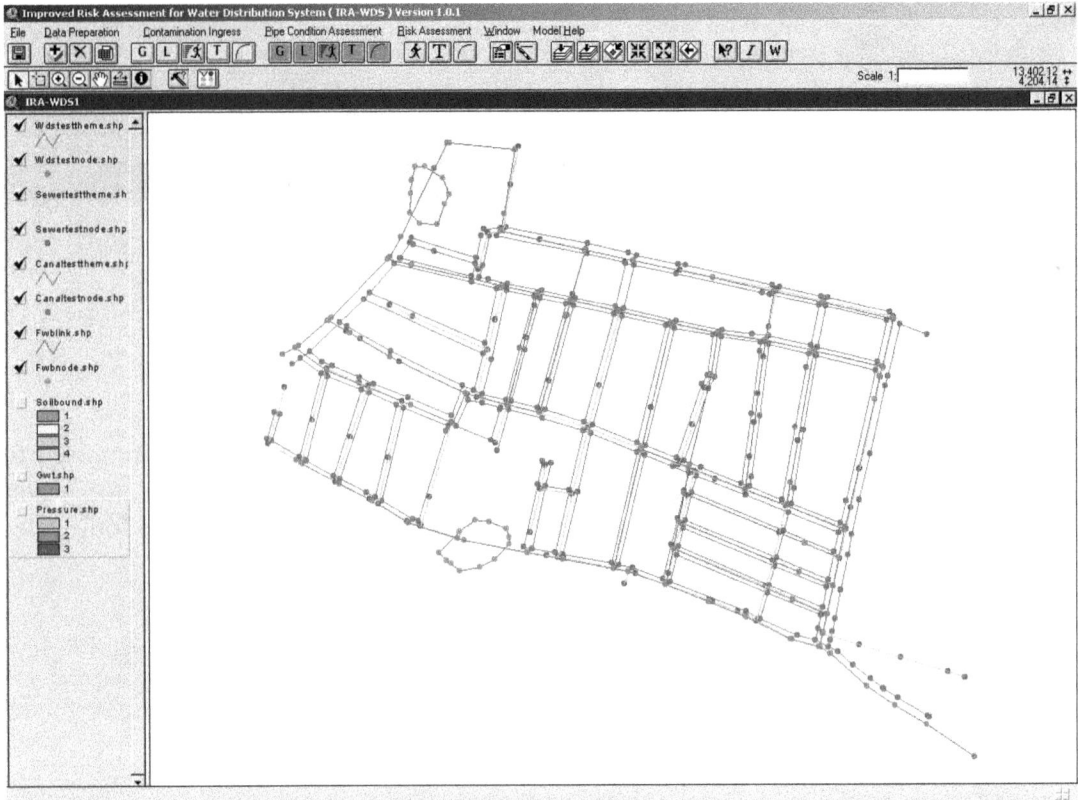

However, if a polygon theme such as soil is to be viewed with these themes, the user should select 'Soilbound.shp'. The view with line and node themes and different soil types is then as below:

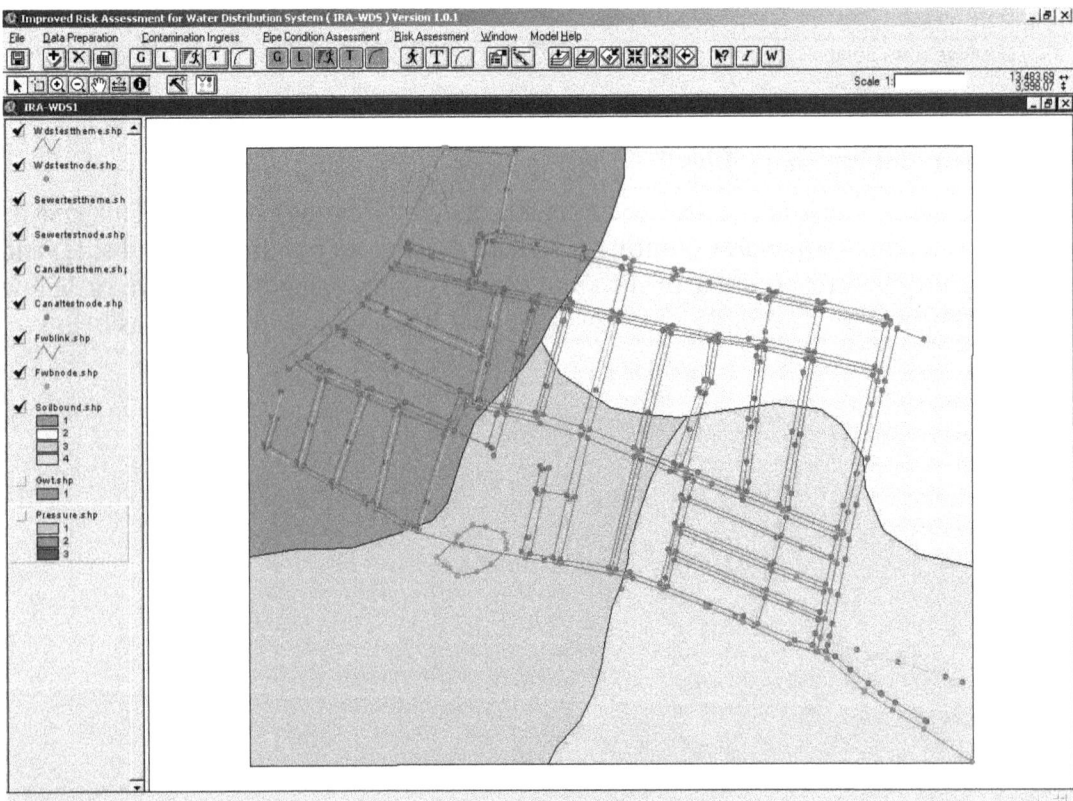

Similarly, if only the water distribution network theme is to be viewed, the user should select '*wdstesttheme.shp*' and '*wdstestnode.shp*', as shown below:

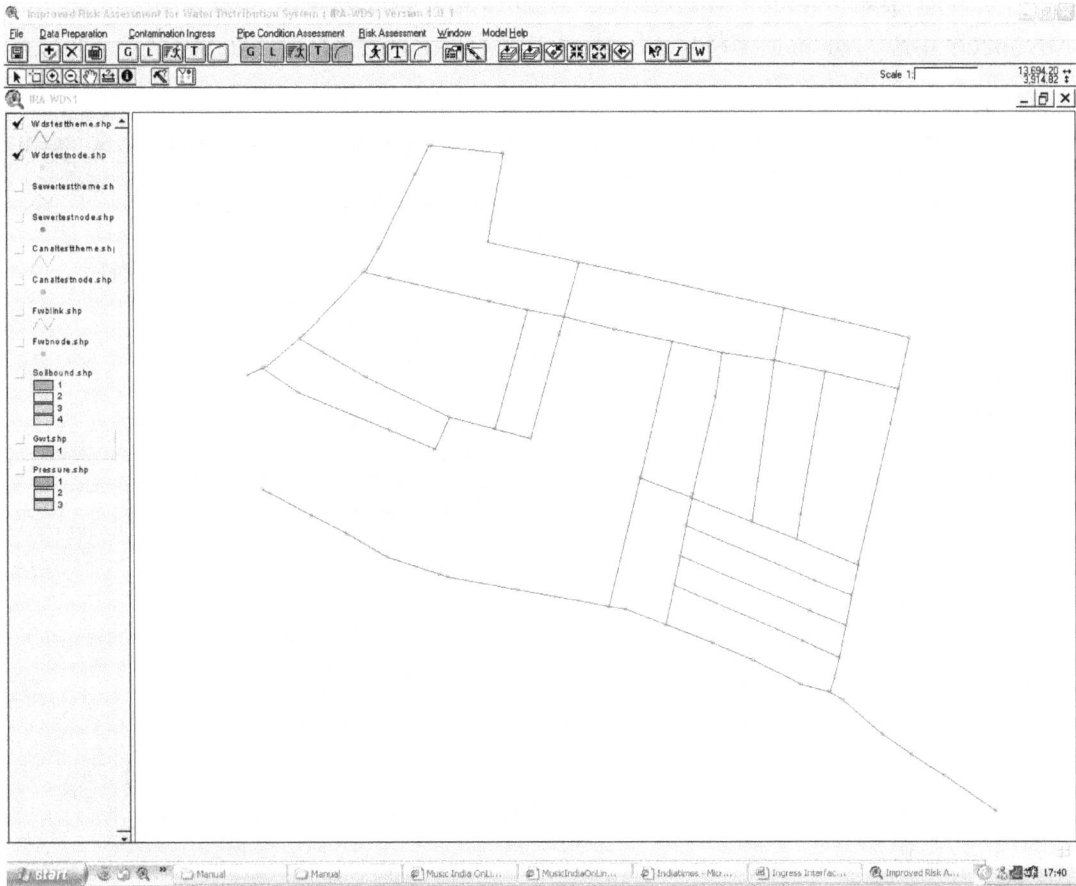

3.3 Generating an input file

3.3.1 Background to Contaminant Ingress Model input

An input file can be generated by clicking on the Tool icon $\boxed{G}$ which is just below the 'Contamination Ingress' menu or by clicking on the 'Contamination Ingress' menu and then clicking on the submenu 'Generate Input File', as shown in the screen below:

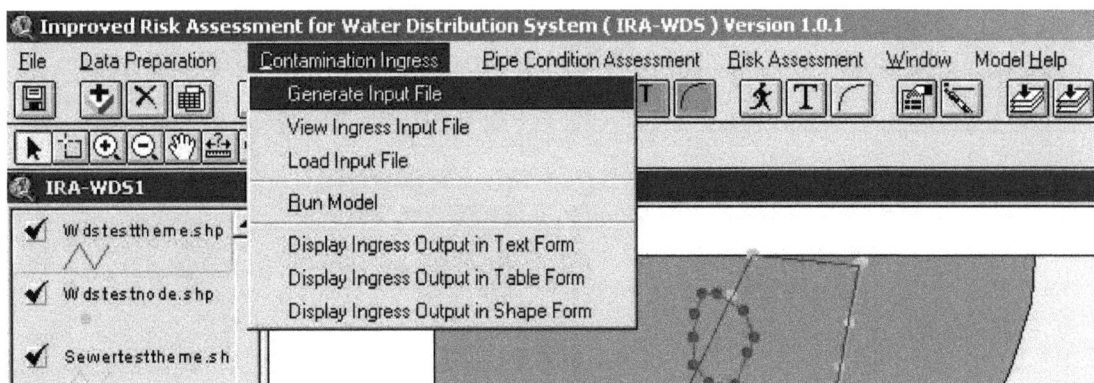

The Contamination Ingress Input Form has two radio button options: **Advanced User** and **End User**.

Advanced users can click on the radio button next to Advanced User/Developer, which allows the user to add or remove fields to or from the 'SELECTED FIELDS' list box. The user can click the ‌Make Default‌ button to select the default field names. Advanced users can add fields to the 'SELECTED FIELDS' list box by selecting those fields in the 'FIELDS AVAILABLE' list box and then clicking on ‌>>‌ button, or can remove fields from the 'SELECTED FIELDS' list box by selecting those fields in the 'SELECTED FIELDS' list and then clicking on ‌<<‌ button.

End users are not provided with the option of adding or deleting fields to or from the 'SELECTED FIELDS' list box. With the End User option, the fields are selected automatically.

3.3.2 Adding shape files

3.3.2.1 Water and sewer distribution data

The themes added by the user in the IRA-WDS View need to be defined in terms of which theme represents what (that is, the user needs to define which theme represents water distribution system pipe/node theme, sewer pipe/node theme, canal link/node theme and foul water body (polygon) link/node theme). All polyline shape files in the IRA-WDS View are listed in each combo box placed under the 'LINK DATA' so that user can choose each respective theme from the list to represent WATER PIPE, SEWER PIPE, CANAL LINK and POLYGON LINK in the IRA-WDS View. All point shape files in the IRA-WDS View are listed in each combo box placed under the 'NODE DATA' so that user can choose each respective theme from the list to represent WATER PIPE NODE, SEWER PIPE NODE, CANAL NODE and POLYGON NODE in the IRA-WDS View.

3.3.2.2 Soil data

SOIL DATA for Contamination Ingress can be defined either through the soil theme, through manual input or through the soil database built within IRA-WDS. All polygon shape files in the IRA-WDS View are listed in combo box placed under the 'SOIL DATA' so that user can choose each respective theme from the list to represent SOIL DATA THEME in the IRA-WDS View.

3.3.2.3 Soil data from theme

The figure below shows the user how to select soil data from the shape files.

3.3.2.4 Soil data manual input

With the soil data manual entry option, the user inputs the soil data desired in a box provided before each soil parameter, as shown below:

3.3.2.5 Soil data from database

With the soil data from database option, the user chooses the soil type from the Soil Type menu, which consists of different soil properties. The user can also modify the soil properties by using the empty boxes next to some soil properties. The some soil properties depend on the interaction of different soils with contaminants (for example, fraction organic content). The user is required to input the values of these properties.

3.4 Generating the input file for the model

After completing the data definition, the next step is for the user to generate the input file to run the Contamination Ingress Model. The Contamination Ingress input file is generated by clicking on the 'Generate Input' button on the 'Contamination Ingress Input Form'. For example, if the soil theme is selected, a spatial analysis is performed by the program to identify the pipes and corresponding soil types in which they are buried; then the soil data is appended according to the node themes of the water distribution system, sewer system, canal and foul water body. Then the user opens the 'File Save' dialogue box to save the file with a user-defined name, as below:

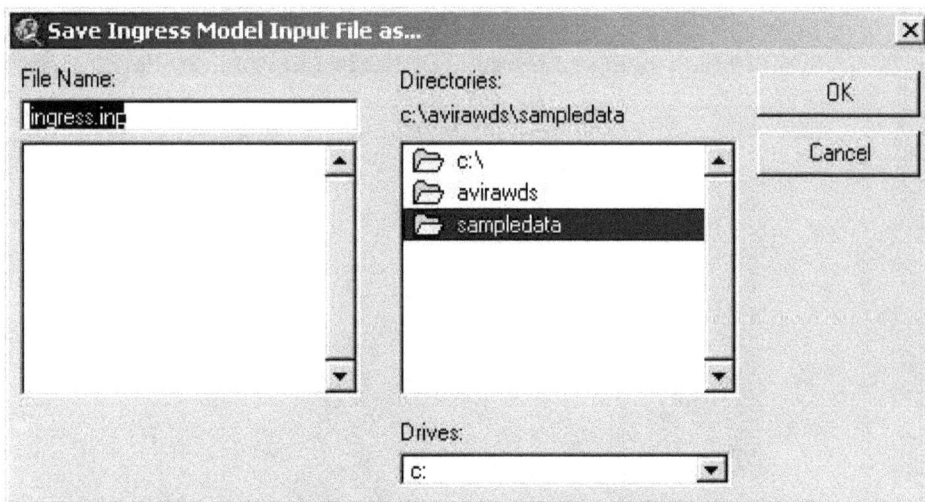

The data generation and writing progress is shown in the Progress Bar as below:

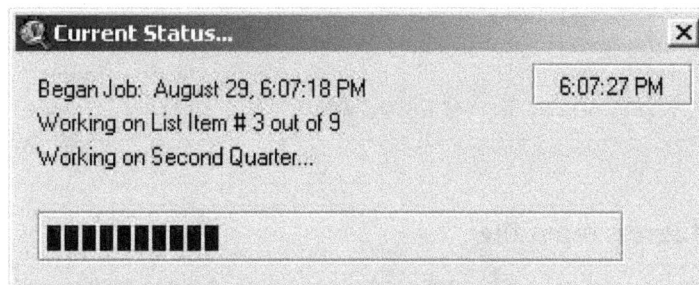

Before the completion of data writing, the model prompts an Input box asking for 'Time of Analysis' (See Appendix B) as shown on next page.

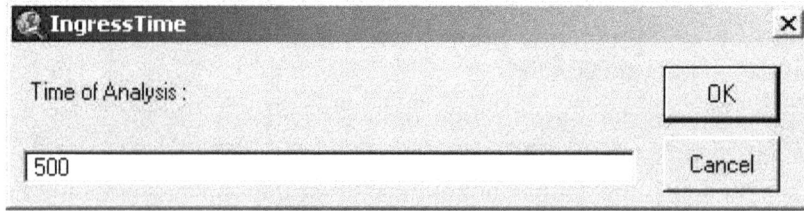

After successfully generating the input file, an Info Message box indicating task completion is displayed as shown below:

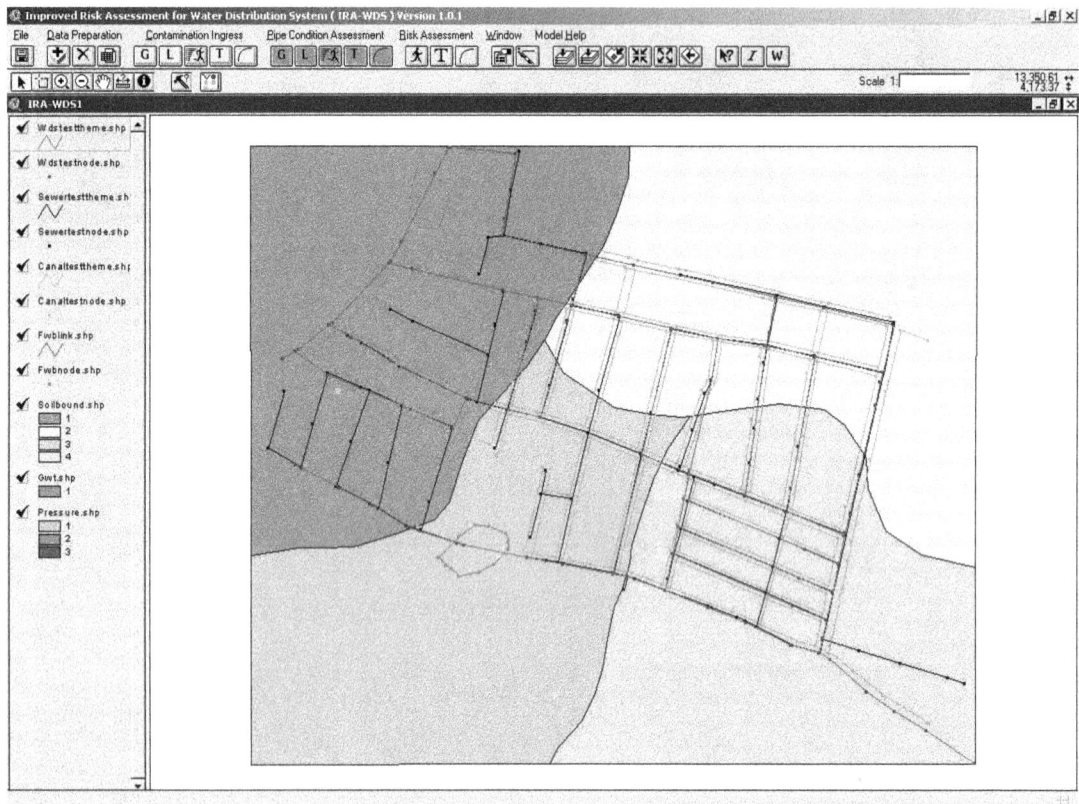

3.4.1 Viewing Ingress input file

The user can view the input file in the notepad by clicking on the [T] button and browsing the appropriate output file to view.

IRA-WDS data viewer

3.4.2 Loading input file

The input file to be used for running the Contaminant Ingress Model is loaded using tool [L] which is just below the 'Contamination Ingress' menu or by clicking on the 'Contamination Ingress' menu and then clicking on the submenu 'Load Input File', as shown on the screen below:

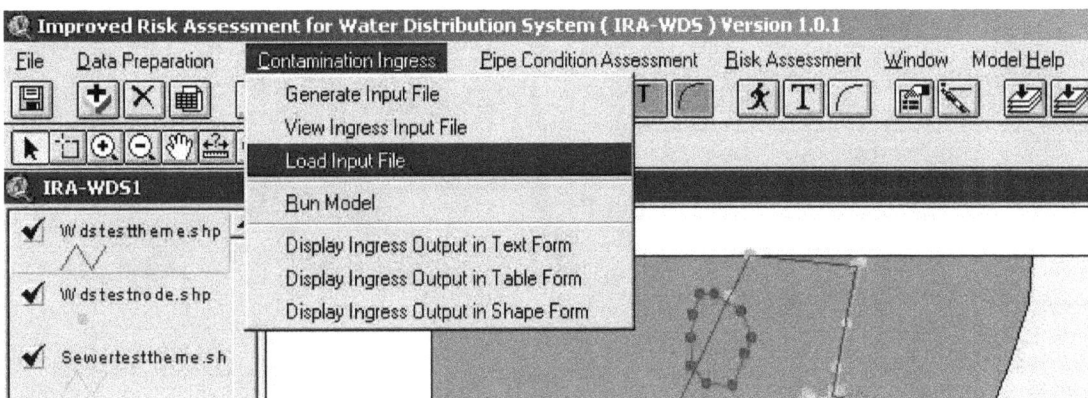

The 'Load Contamination Ingress Input File' dialogue box is as shown below:

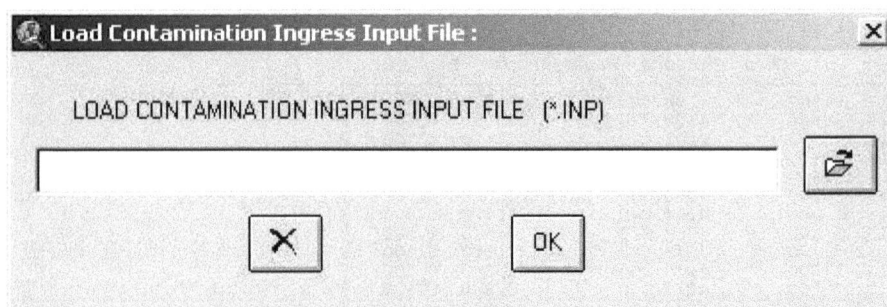

The user can browse through the computer by clicking on the ![folder] button on the 'Load Contamination Ingress Input File' dialogue box. This opens the 'File Load' dialogue box, as shown below:

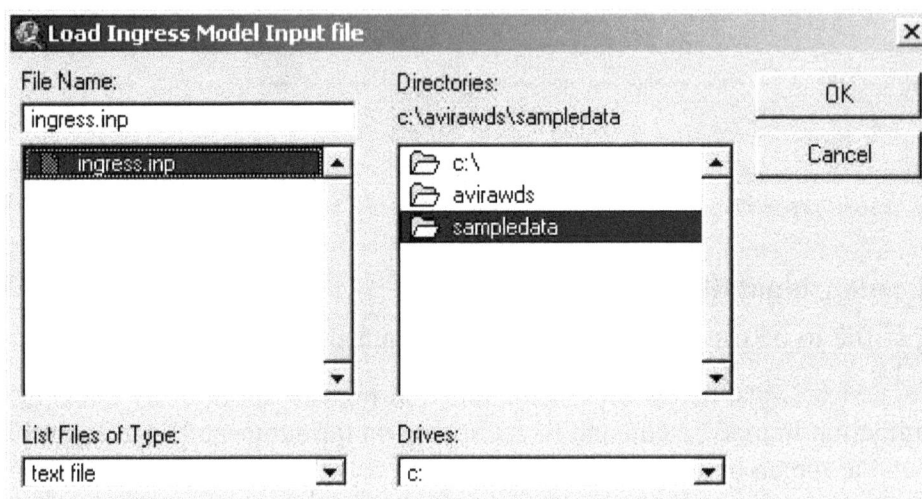

After the appropriate file has been selected, the user presses the 'OK' button on the 'Load Contamination Ingress Input File' dialogue box where the filename appears.

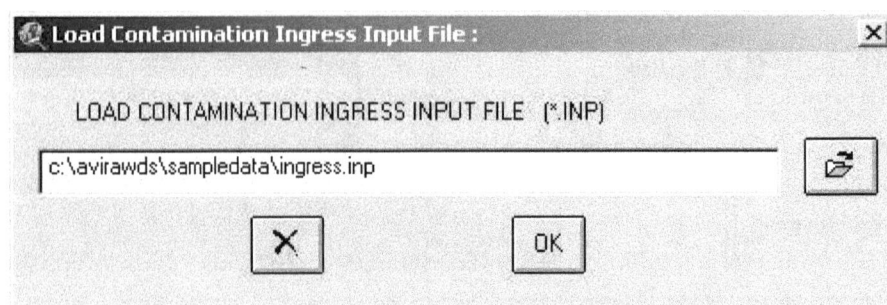

If the user wants to change the filename, he or she can do this by clicking the button ![X], which clears the filename from the 'Load Contamination Ingress Input File' dialogue box. If user is sure of the input file selected, then the file can be loaded by clicking on the ![OK] button, which also closes 'Load Contamination Ingress Input File' dialogue box.

3.5 Running the Contaminant Ingress Model

To run the model, the user clicks on the [icon] button, which is just below the 'Contamination Ingress' menu or he or she clicks on the 'Contamination Ingress' menu and then clicks on the submenu 'Run Model', as shown on the screen below:

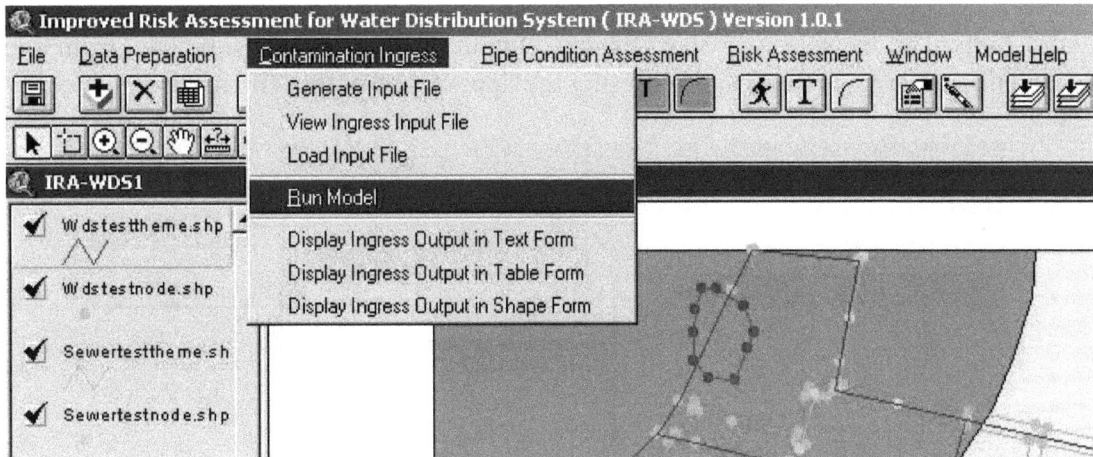

This opens the 'File Save' dialogue box for saving the Contamination Ingress Model output file as *.out. Once the user types the appropriate name and clicks 'OK', then the outputs are generated as specified by the user.

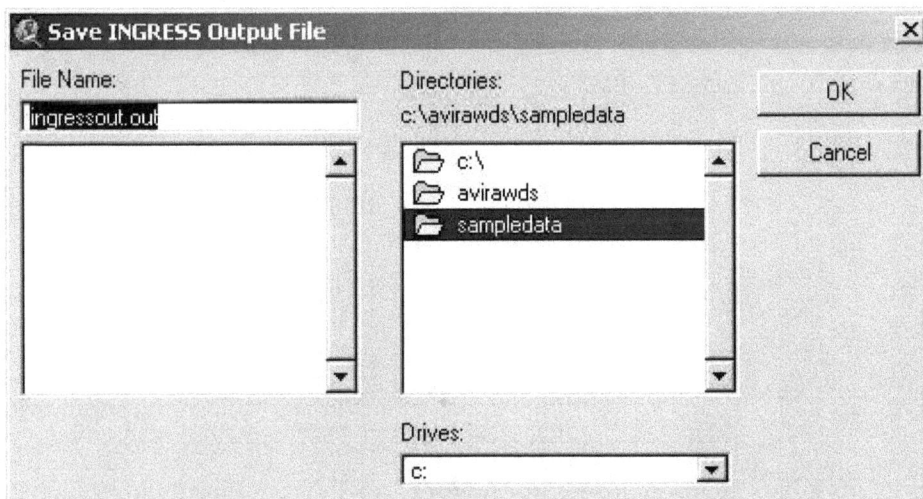

The program then displays the 'Task Completed' Result Message Box, as shown below:

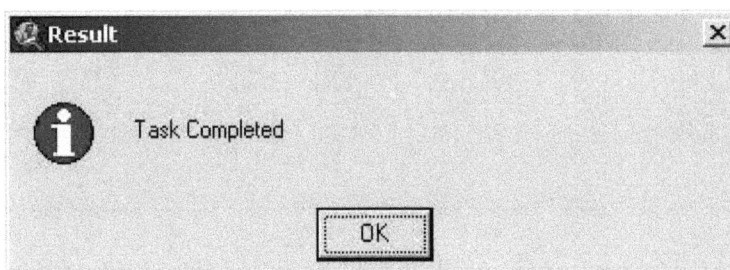

3.6 Displaying output

Outputs can be displayed in text, table and shape forms

3.6.1 Displaying Ingress output in text form

The user can view the output file in text form using the notepad by clicking on the
[T] button or by selecting the Display Output in Text Form submenu from the
Contaminant Ingress menu and browsing the appropriate output file to view.

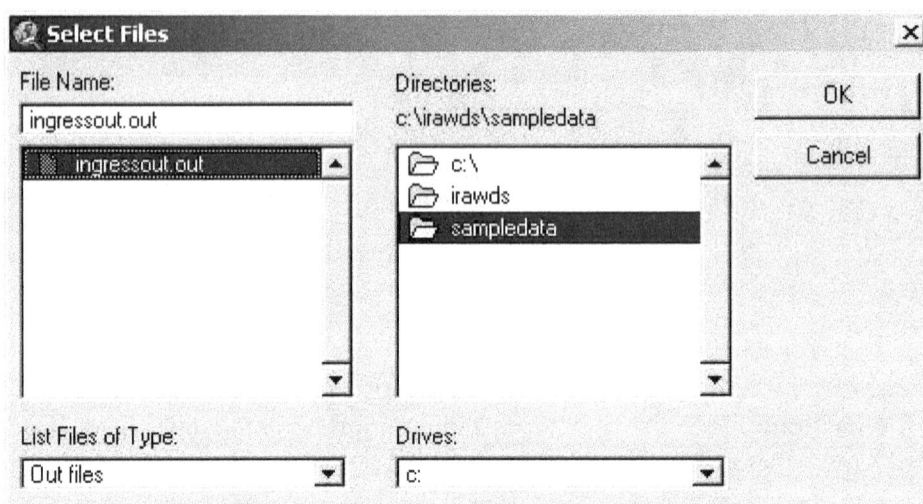

Select Files

File Name: ingressout.out

Directories: c:\irawds\sampledata

- ingressout.out
- c:\
- irawds
- sampledata

OK   Cancel

List Files of Type: Out files

Drives: c:

ingressout - Notepad
File Edit Format Help

```
13340.758680   4190.321166   19.333008   13341.110397   4191.574810   19.334759   0.000034   0.000077   Canal
13418.368612   4163.516650   21.838559   13418.623356   4164.590701   21.815741   0.000120   0.000000   Canal
13496.853542   4134.262668   22.796015   13496.693315   4133.155405   22.817849   0.000000   0.000686   Canal
13529.161266   4121.743106   21.658359   13528.964546   4120.646657   21.622297   0.017711   0.005003   Canal
13525.094990   4097.167669   22.993632   13526.474934   4096.605357   23.006894   0.000608   0.012341   Canal
13519.411532   4076.810376   22.577268   13520.790811   4076.247920   22.614507   0.000000   0.006365   Canal
13513.723859   4056.224104   21.931451   13515.099052   4055.645675   21.981728   0.000000   0.001594   Canal
13454.729409   4125.840851   22.317382   13456.115045   4125.276220   22.330699   0.000399   1.000000   Canal
13449.627867   4105.267464   20.693190   13451.010928   4104.703466   20.730531   0.000182   1.000000   Canal
13444.479030   4085.349627   19.399876   13445.855571   4084.770631   19.450202   0.000032   1.000000   Canal
13605.245850   4258.114835   19.012774   13606.684598   4257.765678   18.982180   0.688059   0.000060   Canal
13596.993322   4223.117301   23.806680   13598.437265   4222.790212   23.887144   0.000000   0.000020   Canal
13568.368461   4102.373289   24.176186   13569.758514   4101.823194   24.268136   0.000000   0.001594   Canal
13563.589873   4081.481496   23.899613   13564.980591   4080.914798   23.948169   0.000003   0.004435   Canal
13558.979699   4060.674813   23.544340   13560.370340   4060.107719   23.575166   0.000012   0.001180   Canal
13554.224723   4039.188709   23.216133   13555.611749   4038.605299   23.253800   0.000016   0.025417   Canal
13436.413689   4063.838759   21.846476   13436.013422   4061.924609   22.061095   0.000000   0.000000   Canal
13396.020955   4074.283895   22.567850   13396.596361   4076.589519   22.544437   0.000000   0.000000   Canal
13439.023035   4250.599793   19.988474   13439.560761   4252.866948   19.940308   1.000000   0.000031   Canal
13475.711054   4245.901606   19.964995   13475.340332   4243.508802   20.002228   0.000026   0.001287   Canal
13512.215721   4240.424314   20.702638   13511.859203   4237.960567   20.751220   0.000118   1.000000   Canal
13548.872185   4231.596323   21.231099   13548.465212   4229.328202   21.251838   0.000094   0.154200   Canal
13416.544162   4156.519432   21.732788   13417.007334   4158.375342   21.713942   0.031755   0.000050   Canal
13453.166507   4143.943882   22.875592   13453.165566   4143.939386   22.875423   0.001111   0.000034   Canal
13512.664183   4242.971394   20.611602   13513.505958   4247.142677   20.407679   0.001387   0.000000   Canal
13455.026644   4151.795708   22.797505   13454.399414   4149.286621   22.890001   0.000000   0.001798   Canal
13454.399414   4149.286621   22.890001   13454.253599   4148.703246   22.906672   0.002154   0.002740   Canal
13281.286043   4203.456051   18.905238   13277.294949   4205.317683   18.941235   0.000025   0.001226   Canal
13310.852755   4327.153069   18.424261   13310.470234   4325.072567   18.427347   0.000066   0.000075   Canal
13518.987586   4274.306022   19.079731   13519.357776   4276.140442   18.990051   1.000000   0.000000   Canal
13364.061789   4273.347555   19.424896   13364.578226   4275.141112   19.390870   0.000205   0.000000   Canal
13453.125537   4143.748028   22.868223   13452.826841   4142.320133   22.814495   0.006760   0.000016   Canal
13469.294867   4208.872357   20.693405   13468.477326   4205.601977   20.813966   0.000065   1.000000   Canal
13468.477932   4205.604400   20.813877   13465.682554   4194.422152   21.226104   0.000028   0.000814   Canal
13452.953942   4142.927732   22.837357   13450.176031   4129.648129   22.337680   0.000608   0.000399   Canal
13450.176004   4129.648004   22.337675   13449.799805   4127.849609   22.270006   0.026995   1.000000   Canal
13449.799805   4127.849609   22.270006   13445.882559   4109.114937   20.753102   0.000399   0.000478   Canal
13449.799805   4127.849609   22.270006   13450.809261   4127.438267   22.279708   0.000399   1.000000   Canal
13445.882559   4109.114937   20.753102   13445.435547   4106.977051   20.580002   1.000000   0.164289   Canal
13445.435547   4106.977051   20.580002   13444.662755   4103.282502   20.342801   0.000478   0.000066   Canal
13445.435547   4106.977051   20.580002   13445.587174   4106.915219   20.584096   0.000478   1.000000   Canal
13256.022229   4364.452895   18.608311   13257.847819   4368.020144   18.615253   0.080125   0.080125   waterbody1
13253.787176   4360.085543   18.599811   13256.022229   4364.452895   18.608311   0.024923   0.024923   waterbody1
13251.098302   4354.831415   18.589586   13253.787176   4360.085543   18.599811   0.010150   0.010150   waterbody1
13248.116713   4349.005315   18.578247   13251.098302   4354.831415   18.589586   0.004756   0.004756   waterbody1
13242.523188   4338.075422   18.556976   13248.116713   4349.005315   18.578247   0.002437   0.002437   waterbody1
13241.432843   4335.944861   18.552829   13242.523188   4338.075422   18.556976   0.001331   0.001331   waterbody1
13275.857696   4094.567293   22.330763   13275.911133   4094.550537   22.330000   0.001764   0.001764   waterbody2
13272.907992   4095.492210   22.372913   13275.857696   4094.567293   22.330763   0.000104   0.000104   waterbody2
13280.657952   4093.062239   22.320739   13281.037109   4092.943359   22.320000   0.000011   0.000011   waterbody2
13275.911133   4094.550537   22.330000   13280.657952   4093.062239   22.320739   0.000002   0.000002   waterbody2
13308.210487   4087.988766   22.275919   13312.870158   4087.139156   22.268360   0.000000   0.000000   waterbody2
13301.504856   4089.211422   22.286797   13308.210487   4087.988766   22.275919   0.000000   0.000000   waterbody2
13294.962001   4090.404397   22.297411   13301.504856   4089.211422   22.286797   0.000000   0.000000   waterbody2
13286.262740   4091.990556   22.311523   13294.962001   4090.404397   22.297411   0.000000   0.000000   waterbody2
13281.037109   4092.943359   22.320000   13286.262740   4091.990556   22.311523   0.000000   0.000000   waterbody2
```

3.6.2 Displaying Ingress output in table form

The user can view the output file in table form by selecting the Display Output in Table Form submenu from the Contaminant Ingress menu and specifying the appropriate output file to view by browsing as below:

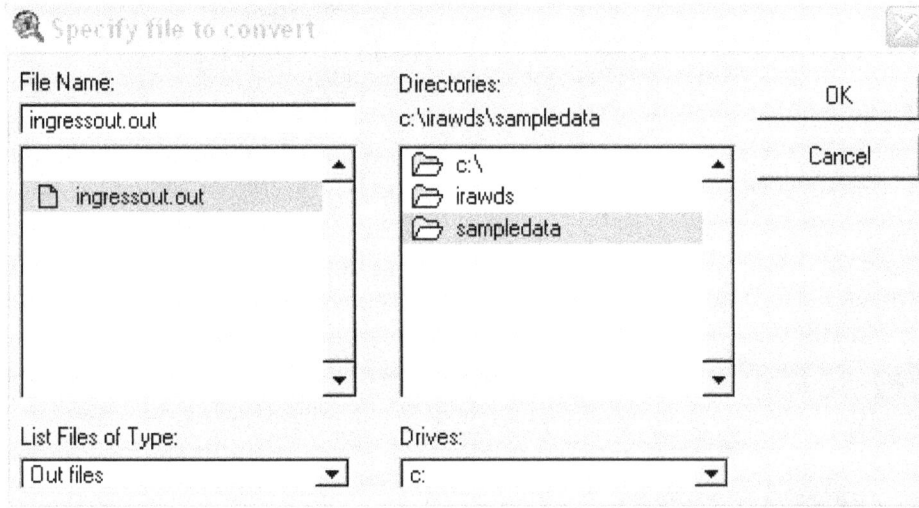

PipeID	StartX	StartY	StartZ	EndX	EndY	EndZ	StartConc	EndConc	C...
898	13529.700	4237.970	20.929	13547.300	4234.320	21.181	0.383	1.000	Sewer
894	13512.400	4241.870	20.665	13512.500	4242.250	20.647	1.000	0.000	Sewer
865	13609.600	4257.060	18.920	13610.100	4256.940	18.910	1.000	0.000	Sewer
914	13605.700	4238.720	21.605	13610.100	4256.940	18.910	1.000	0.000	Sewer
917	13175.500	4220.390	19.550	13175.700	4220.280	19.554	0.000	0.039	Sewer
808	13374.600	4309.420	18.739	13374.800	4309.380	18.737	1.000	0.000	Sewer
842	13520.100	4277.900	18.912	13520.500	4277.810	18.924	0.000	1.000	Sewer
1151	13559.000	4009.350	22.300	13559.000	4009.350	22.300	0.016	1.000	Canal
1151	13559.100	4009.290	22.302	13559.100	4009.290	22.302	0.000	0.046	Canal
1143	13553.600	4015.390	21.916	13554.100	4017.120	21.724	0.000	0.000	Canal
809	13230.400	4301.180	18.492	13228.800	4301.540	18.487	0.000	0.000	Canal
879	13184.300	4252.940	18.787	13182.900	4253.710	18.765	0.000	0.000	Canal
917	13157.900	4232.040	19.135	13159.300	4231.150	19.167	0.000	0.002	Canal
836	13373.500	4306.110	18.803	13373.900	4307.420	18.778	0.025	0.000	Canal
855	13362.600	4268.160	19.444	13362.900	4269.390	19.446	0.000	0.000	Canal
944	13337.900	4275.000	19.733	13337.600	4273.700	19.721	0.000	0.000	Canal
944	13316.200	4197.820	19.021	13315.900	4196.530	19.009	0.002	0.000	Canal
950	13340.800	4190.320	19.333	13341.100	4191.570	19.335	0.000	0.000	Canal
975	13418.400	4163.520	21.839	13418.600	4164.590	21.816	0.000	0.000	Canal
1016	13496.900	4134.260	22.796	13496.700	4133.160	22.818	0.000	0.001	Canal
1029	13529.200	4121.740	21.658	13529.000	4120.650	21.622	0.018	0.005	Canal
1064	13525.100	4097.170	22.994	13526.500	4096.610	23.007	0.001	0.012	Canal
1085	13519.400	4076.810	22.577	13520.800	4076.250	22.615	0.000	0.006	Canal
1107	13513.700	4056.220	21.932	13515.100	4055.650	21.982	0.000	0.002	Canal
1064	13454.700	4125.840	22.317	13456.100	4125.280	22.331	0.000	1.000	Canal
1085	13449.600	4105.270	20.693	13451.000	4104.700	20.730	0.000	1.000	Canal
1107	13444.500	4085.350	19.400	13445.900	4084.770	19.450	0.000	1.000	Canal
865	13605.200	4258.110	19.013	13606.700	4257.770	18.982	0.688	0.000	Canal
915	13597.000	4223.120	23.807	13598.400	4222.790	23.887	0.000	0.000	Canal
1047	13568.400	4102.370	24.176	13569.800	4101.820	24.268	0.000	0.002	Canal
1078	13563.600	4081.480	23.900	13565.000	4080.910	23.948	0.000	0.004	Canal
1100	13559.000	4060.670	23.544	13560.400	4060.110	23.575	0.000	0.001	Canal
1114	13554.200	4039.190	23.216	13555.600	4038.610	23.254	0.000	0.025	Canal
1097	13436.900	4063.840	21.846	13436.000	4061.920	22.061	0.000	0.000	Canal
1082	13396.000	4074.280	22.568	13396.600	4076.590	22.544	0.000	0.000	Canal
975	13439.000	4250.600	19.988	13439.600	4252.870	19.940	1.000	0.000	Canal
918	13475.700	4245.900	19.965	13475.300	4243.510	20.002	0.000	0.001	Canal
1016	13512.200	4240.420	20.703	13511.900	4237.960	20.751	0.000	1.000	Canal
1012	13548.900	4231.600	21.231	13548.500	4229.330	21.252	0.000	0.154	Canal
1082	13416.500	4156.520	21.733	13417.000	4158.380	21.714	0.032	0.000	Canal
1019	13453.200	4143.940	22.876	13453.200	4143.940	22.875	0.001	0.000	Canal
884	13512.700	4242.970	20.612	13513.500	4247.140	20.408	0.001	0.000	Canal
989	13455.000	4151.800	22.797	13454.400	4149.290	22.890	0.000	0.002	Canal
993	13454.400	4149.290	22.890	13454.300	4148.700	22.907	0.002	0.003	Canal
936	13281.300	4203.460	18.905	13277.300	4205.320	18.941	0.000	0.001	Canal

3.6.3 Displaying Ingress output in shape form

To view the Contamination Ingress Model output in shape file form click on the button, which is just below the 'Contamination Ingress' menu or by clicking on the 'Contamination Ingress' menu and then clicking on the submenu 'Display Ingress Output in Shape Form', as shown in the screen below:

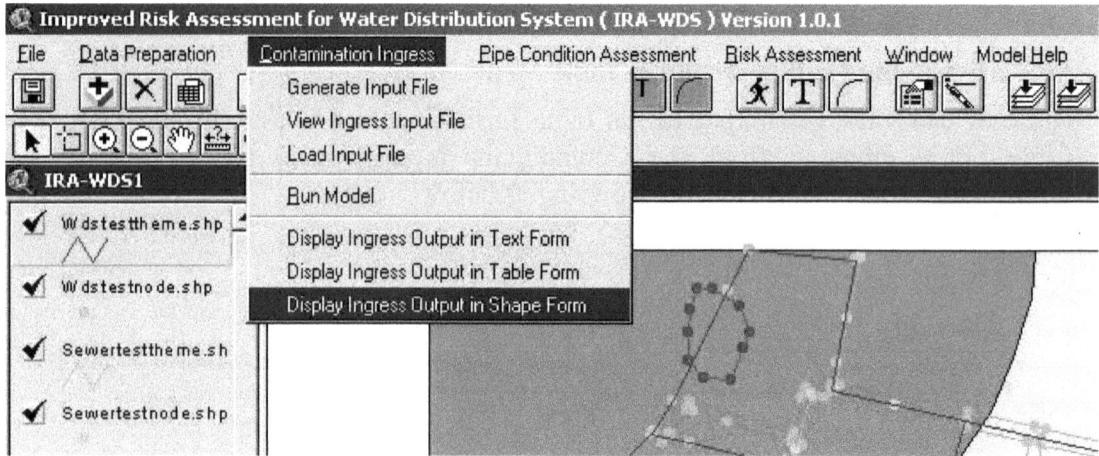

This opens the 'File Select' dialogue box for selecting the Contamination Ingress output file as *.out, which has to be converted to shape file as shown below:

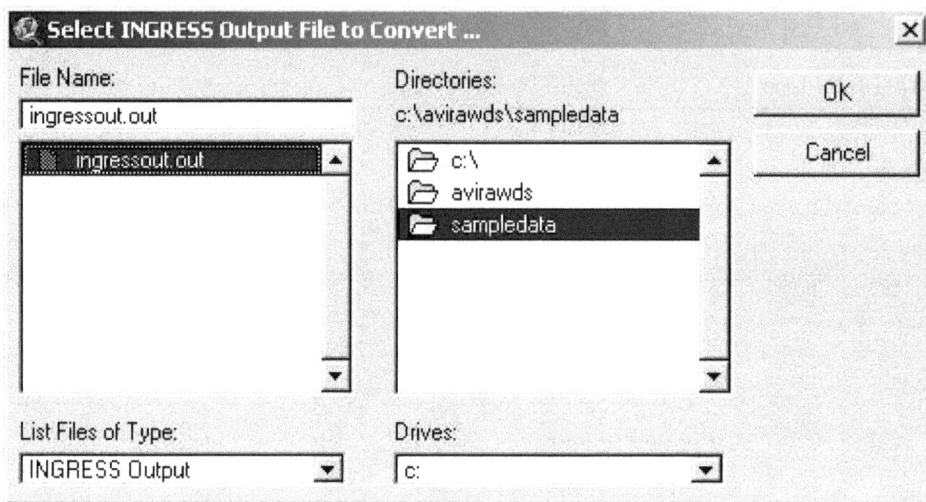

Once the user has selected the appropriate filename and clicked 'OK', this opens the 'File Save' dialogue box and asks the user to type in the output shape filename:

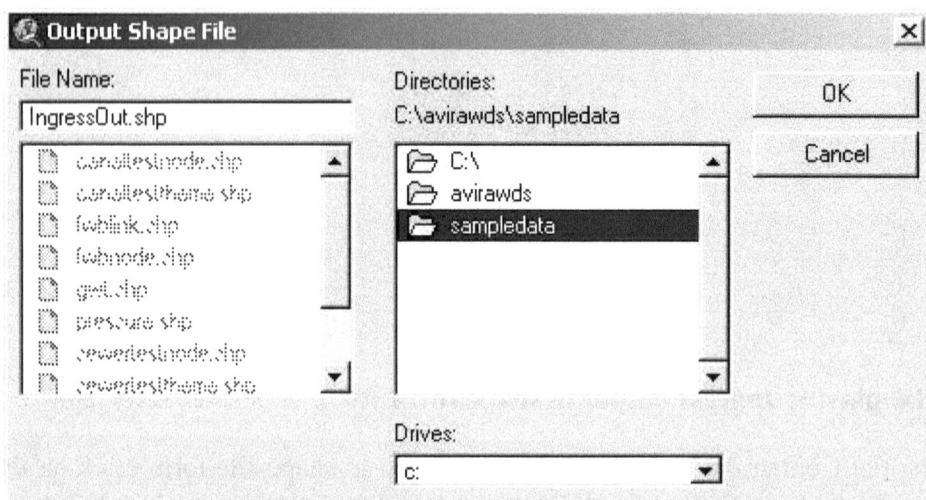

After typing or selecting the appropriate name, the user needs to click the 'OK' button, which then generates the shape file with information from the Contamination

44

Ingress output shape file and loads that file into the IRA-WDS data viewer with contamination legend as shown below:

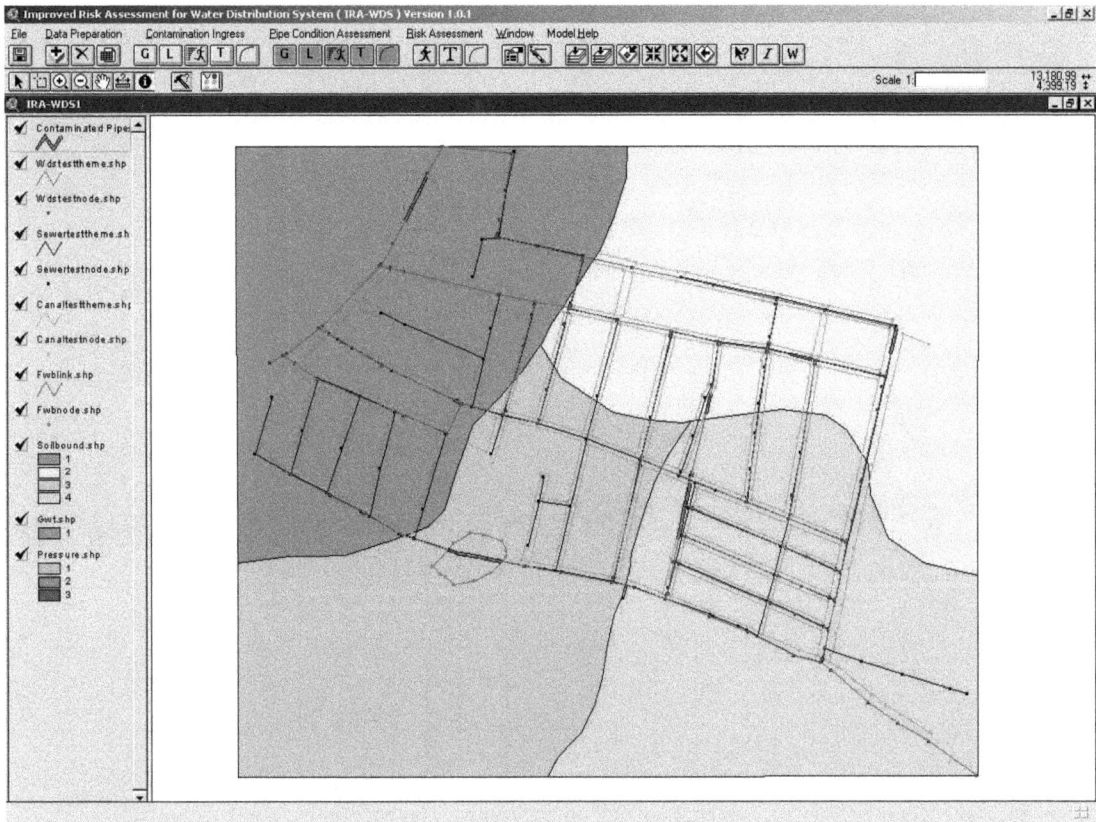

CHAPTER FOUR

Pipe Condition Assessment Model

Chapter-1
IRA-WDS: Overview

Chapter-2
Data Preparation

Chapter-3
Contaminant Ingress Model

Chapter-4
Pipe Condition Assessment Model

Chapter-5
Risk Assessment Model

Chapter 4: Pipe Condition Assessment Model

4.1 Introduction

There are several submenus under the Pipe Condition Assessment menu. This chapter describes the use of these submenus and associated commands for running the Pipe Condition Assessment Model. Figure 4.1 shows the steps involved in executing this component of the software.

The example files given in Table 4.1 are used for illustration purposes to describe the Pipe Condition Assessment Model with the help of IRA-WDS.

Table 4.1. Example input files	
Themes	**Filenames**
Water distribution	wdstesttheme.shp
	wdstestnode.shp
Groundwater	gwt.shp
Pressure zone	pressure.shp
Soil type	soilbound.shp

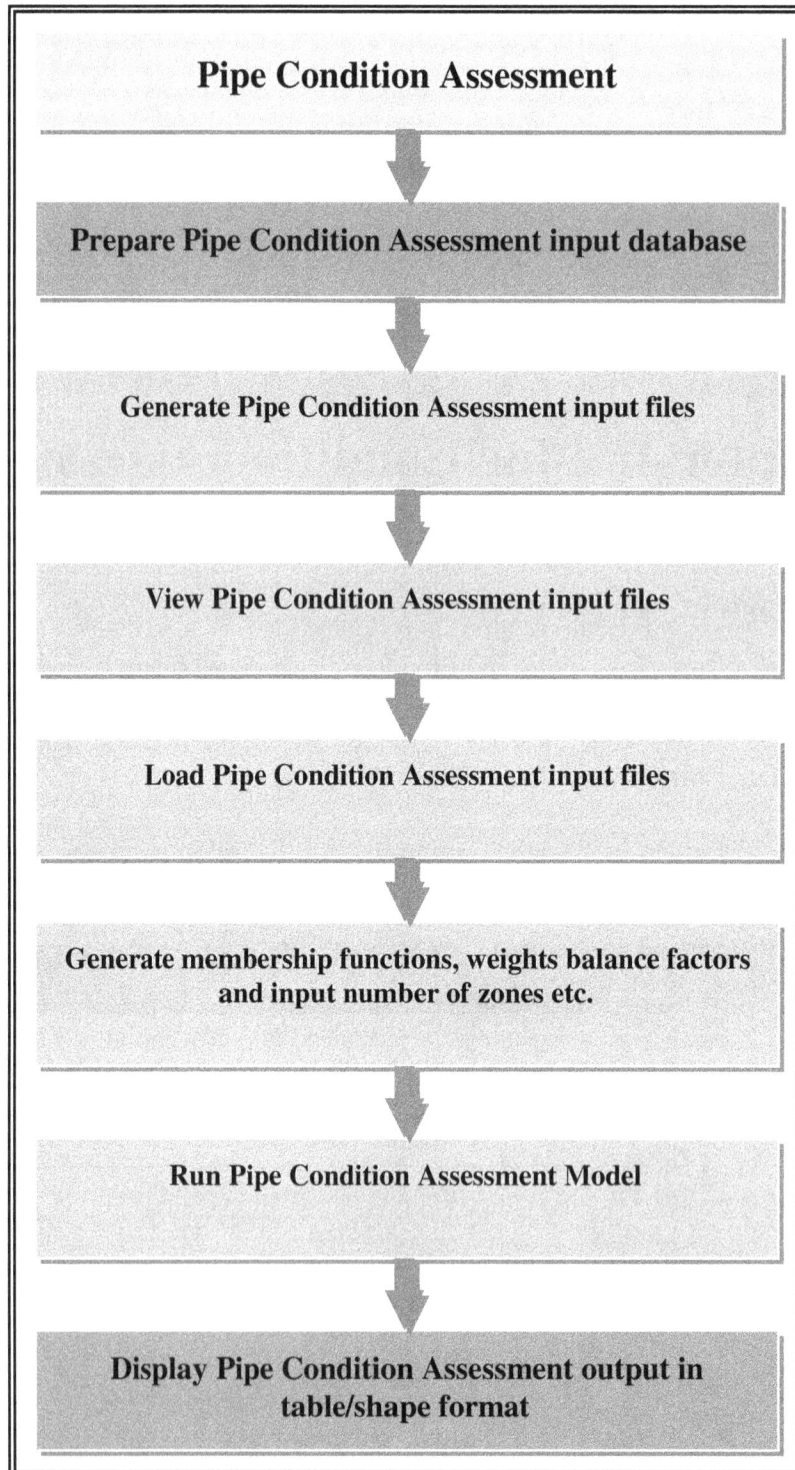

Figure 4.1. Overview of Pipe Condition Assessment Model of IRA-WDS

The following steps need to be performed for running the Pipe Condition Assessment (PCA). These are:

- Adding the data (if not already done so)
- Rearranging the data (optional)
- Generating an input file

- Viewing PCA input file (optional)
- Loading input file
- Running model
- Displaying output (optional)

4.2 Shape files

4.2.1 Adding shape files

Adding shape files can be done by clicking on the Tool icon ⊞ which is just below the 'Data Preparation' menu or by clicking on the 'Data Preparation' menu and then clicking on the submenu 'Add Shape Files to IRA-WDS View', as shown in the screen below:

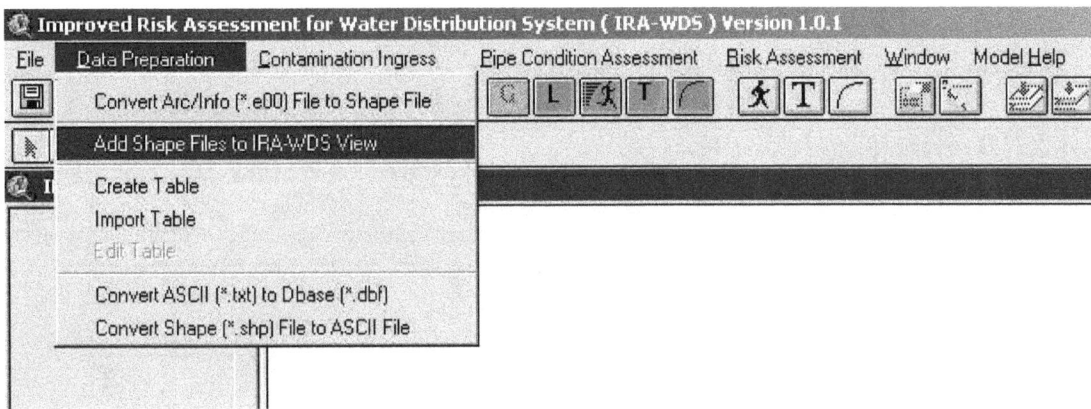

This opens the 'Add Theme' form, as shown below, and the user is then required to select the desired files. At this stage, these files are those relating to: water distribution link and node; soil polygon map; groundwater zone polygon map; and pressure zone polygon map.

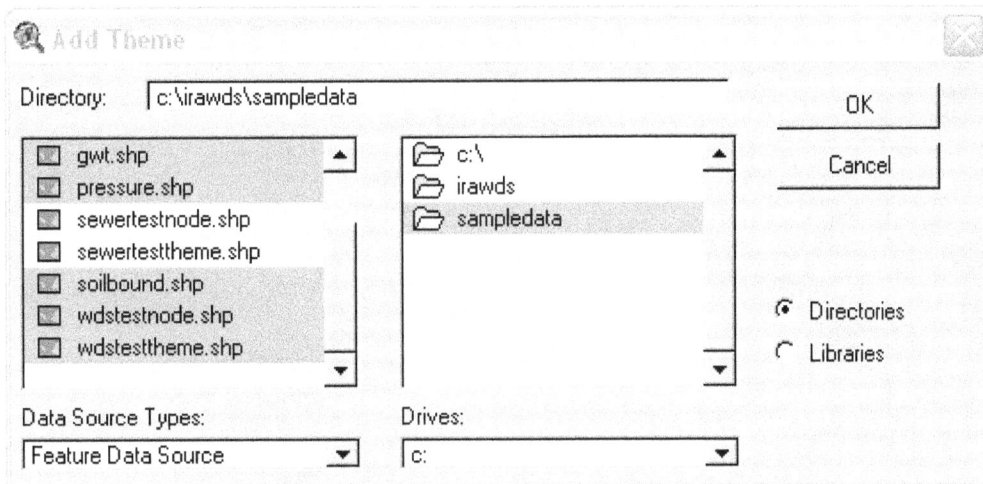

If the user is continuing on from the Contaminant Ingress Model, then water distribution link and node data and the soil polygon map will have already been added. (Note that the sewer pipe, canal and foul water bodies link and node data, which are all needed for pipe condition assessment, will also have been added in this

51

case). Only the groundwater zone polygon map and the pressure zone polygon map need to be added by the user as below.

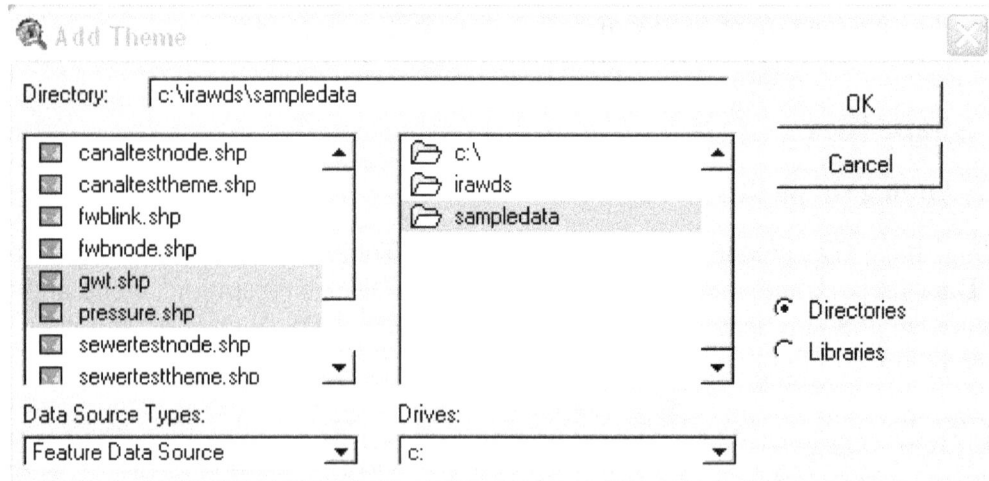

4.2.2 Rearranging shape files

If the user wishes to do so, he or she can rearrange the data to view and query different themes. The following snapshots show:

- Rearranged link and node data
- A soil theme map
- A groundwater theme map
- A pressure theme map

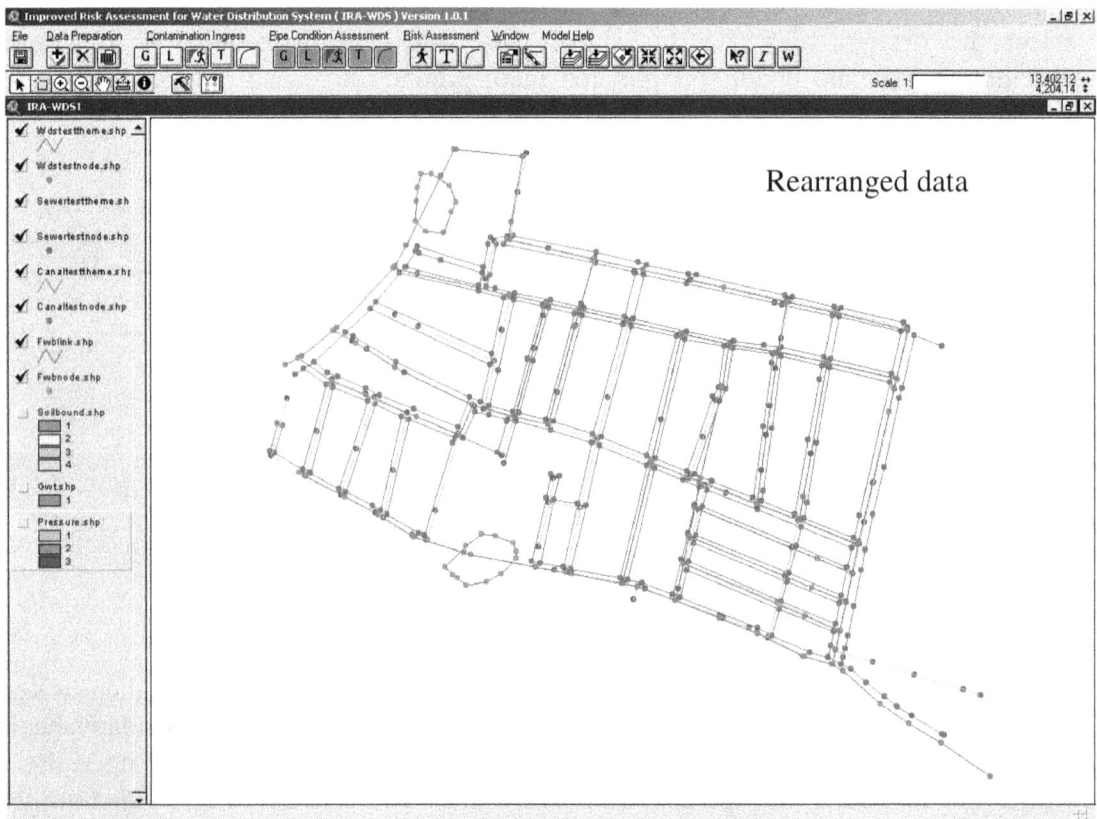

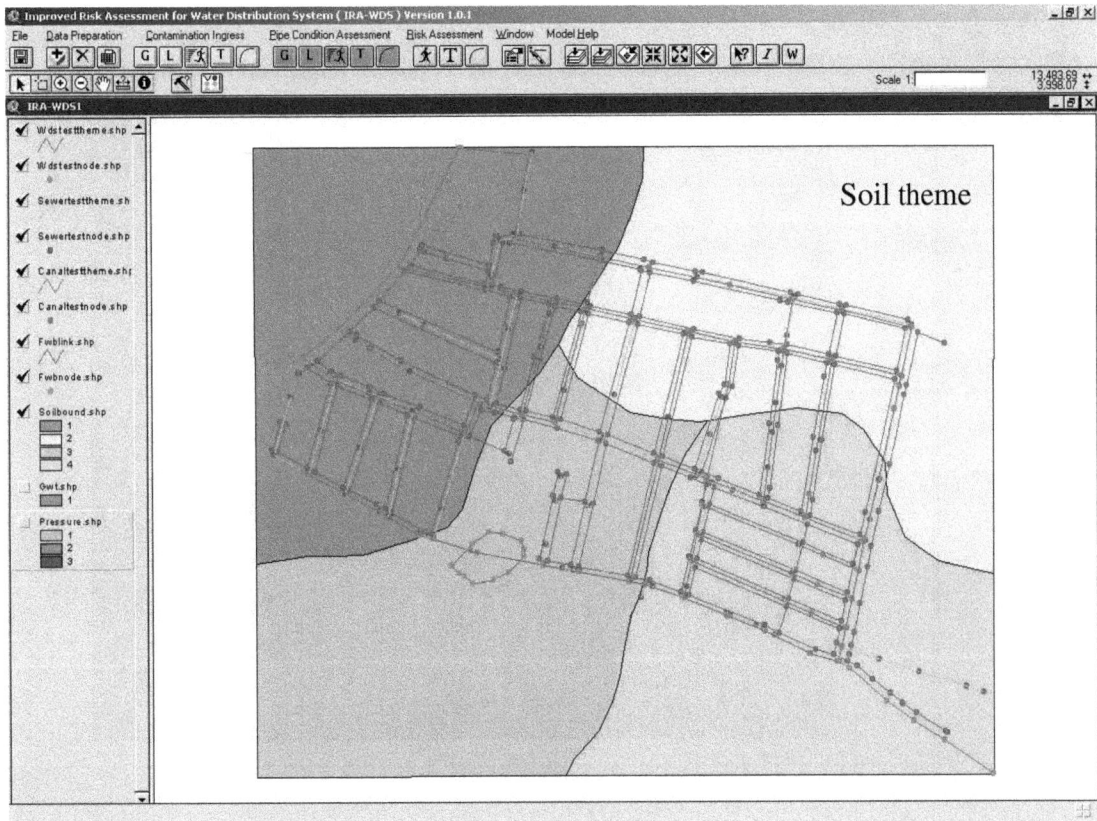

Soil theme

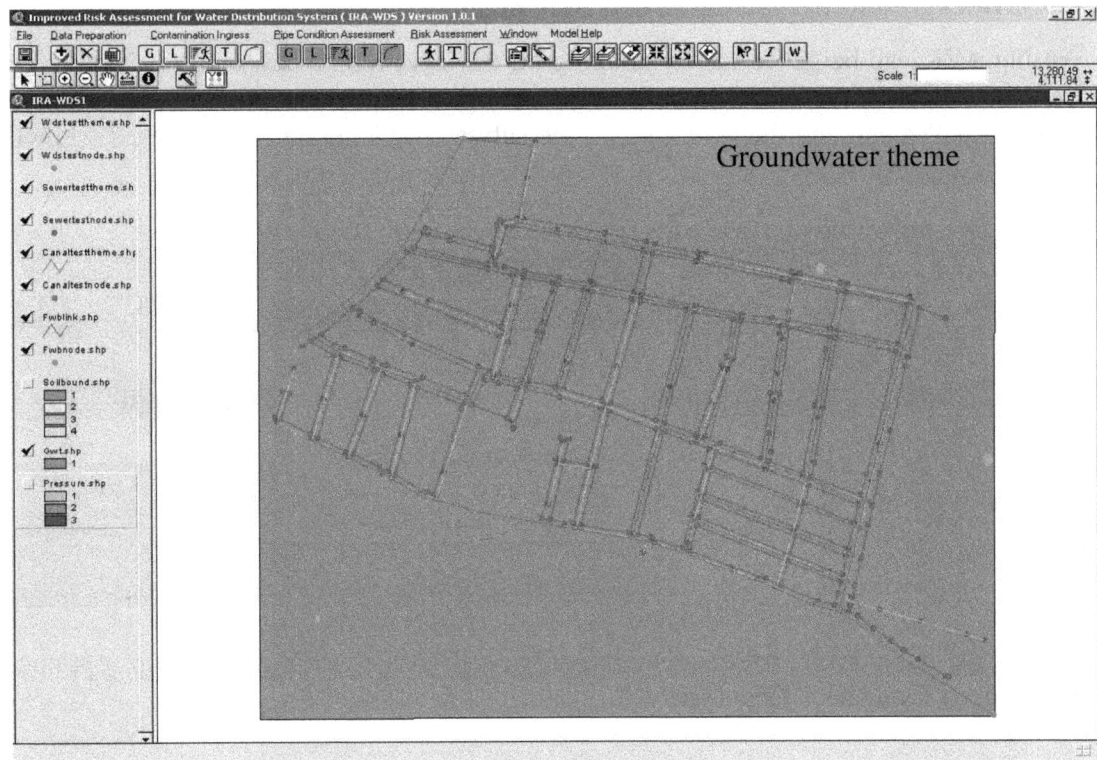

Groundwater theme

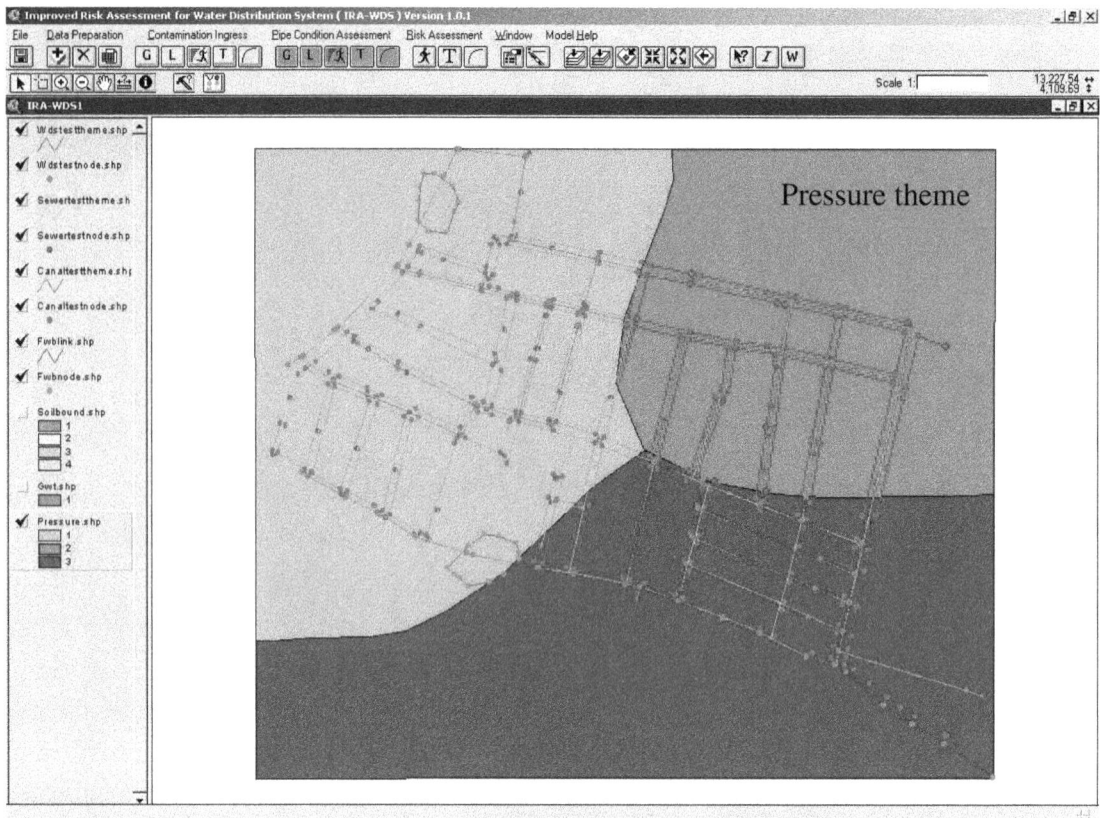

Pressure theme

4.3 Generating an input file

4.3.1 Background to Pipe Condition Assessment Model input

An input file can be generated by clicking on the Tool icon [G] which is just below the 'Pipe Condition Assessment' menu or by clicking on the 'Pipe Condition Assessment' menu and then clicking on the submenu 'Generate Input File', as shown on the screen below:

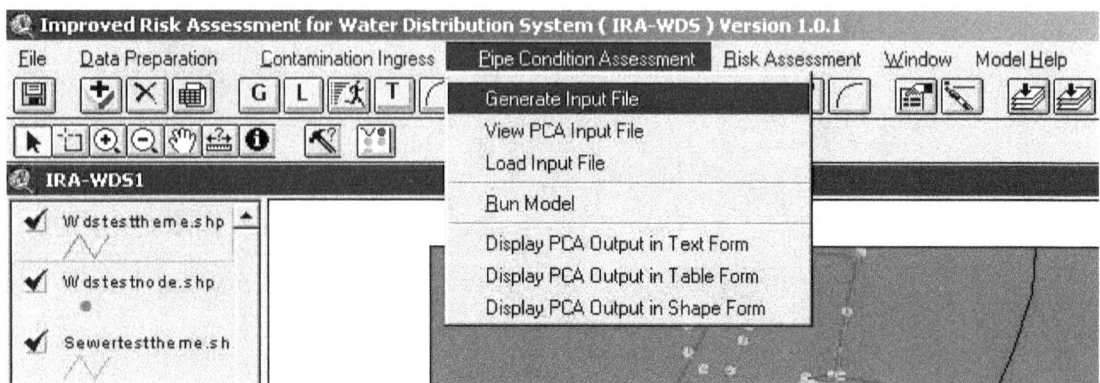

The 'Pipe Condition Assessment Input Form' has two radio button options: '**Advanced User**' and '**End User**'.

Advance Users can click on the radio button next to Advance User / Developer, which will allow the user to add or remove fields to or from the 'SELECTED FIELDS' list box. The user can click the Make Default button to select the default field names. Advanced users can add fields to the 'SELECTED FIELDS' list box by selecting

54

those fields in the 'FIELDS AVAILABLE' list box and then clicking on the ⟩⟩ button. To remove fields from the 'SELECTED FIELDS' list box, the user can select those fields in the 'SELECTED FIELDS' list box and remove by clicking on the ⟨⟨ button.

End Users are not provided with an option for adding or deleting fields to or from the 'SELECTED FIELDS' list box. In this case, the fields are automatically selected with the End User option.

4.3.2 Adding shape files

The user needs to define which theme in the IRA-WDS View represents the water distribution system pipe theme, the node theme, the soil theme, the groundwater theme and the pressure theme. All polyline / line themes added to the IRA-WDS viewer are added to the 'PIPE LINK THEME' combo box. All point / node themes added to the IRA-WDS viewer are added to the 'PIPE NODE THEME' combo box. All polygon themes added to the IRA-WDS viewer are added to the 'SOIL THEME', 'GROUNDWATER THEME' and 'PRESSURE THEME' boxes.

The user is required to select the theme that represents the water distribution pipe theme, the node theme, the soil theme, the groundwater theme and the pressure theme from the combo box. Initially, before selection of the themes, all other menus are disabled. During the selection of themes, the list of fields available and fields that will be selected from that theme are listed in the 'FIELDS AVAILABLE' and 'FIELDS SELECTED' list boxes (just below 'SELECT ATTRUBUTE DATA FROM FIELDS').

4.3.2.1 Pipe (water distribution) link theme

Selecting the water distribution theme in the pipe link theme box lists the fields available and fields selected. It also goes through the first record of the theme and finds which data are available and then enables the further options for data definition accordingly. For example, if the Pipe Diameter has a numeric value in its database, then it enables the Pipe Diameter check box in the Input Form so that the user can choose this for assessing the pipe condition and so on, as shown below:

4.3.2.2 Pipe node (water distribution) theme

Selecting the water distribution theme in the pipe node theme box updates the list of fields available and selected.

4.3.2.3 Soil, groundwater and pressure themes

If any of the soil, groundwater or /pressure themes is already selected, then the check box options corresponding to 'Soil Corrosivity', 'Ground Water Table' or 'Maximum Pressure' will be enabled, or else these options will remain disabled, as shown below:

4.3.2.4 Soil theme

Selecting the soil theme updates the list of available and selected fields. This also enables check box options corresponding to 'Soil Corrosivity' (see screen below). If the water distribution (pipe) node theme is not already selected, then the check box options corresponding to 'Soil Corrosivity' will remain disabled.

4.3.2.5 Groundwater theme

Selecting the groundwater theme updates the list of available and selected fields. This also enables check box options corresponding to 'Ground Water Table' (see screen below). If the water distribution node theme is not already selected, then the check box options corresponding to 'Ground Water Table' will remain disabled.

4.3.2.6 Pressure theme

Selecting the pressure theme updates the list of available and selected fields. This also enables check box options corresponding to 'Maximum Pressure' (see screen below). If the water distribution node theme is not already selected, then the check box options corresponding to 'Maximum Pressure' will remain disabled.

4.4 Indicator data

Depending on the data available on various themes, the options for entering data for the following different indicators will be enable or disenabled.

1. Pipe Indicators
2. Corrosion Indicators
3. Installation Indicators
4. Pipe Failure Indicators
5. Load/Strength Indicators
6. Intermittency Indicators

The user needs to select which parameters of these indicators he or she wants to use for pipe condition assessment. The data used for these parameters are not only quantitative (crisp value data) but also qualitative (fuzzy data). In case of fuzzy data, the user needs to define the membership functions for the fuzzy data sets.

Pipe material
Various material properties are considered while deciding the condition of the pipe. These properties are:

1. Resistance to corrosion (a fuzzy parameter)
2. Maximum pressure it can sustain
3. Maximum impact load it can sustain
4. Minimum and maximum diameters in which pipes are made
5. Minimum and maximum lengths in which pipes are made
6. Maximum design life
7. Age-Hazen-William Roughness Coefficient (C) relationship

The input for pipe material properties is made in two different input forms. After opening the form 'Pipe Material', the user checks the "Assign Material Properties" box (see screen below). This form lists the available pipe materials in the water distribution pipe theme. If the default database for the pipe material in the IRA-WDS contains the pipe material listed in water distribution pipe theme, then it populates the respective fields for those pipe material properties for which data are available; otherwise nothing is written. For example, in the screen below the IRA-WDS database has all the necessary data for the pipe material 'AC' listed in the water distribution pipe theme, hence all the pipe material properties' check boxes are filled. However, for the pipe material 'U1', the IRA-WDS database has no pipe material data and hence all the pipe material properties' check boxes are empty. The user needs to fill in all the empty fields in the form appropriately. He or she can also modify the data if they do not agree with the IRA-WDS default database. An input form having some default data from the database and some material to be defined by the user is shown on next page.

Pipe Material	Corrosion Index	Max. Pressure	Max. Load	Design Life	Max. Diameter	Min. Diameter
AC	Very Strong	35.700	23.500	60	2500.000	50.000
RCC	Very Strong	30.000	30.000	60	1200.000	400.000
U1	Very Strong					
PVC	Very Strong	15.300	4.400	60	1200.000	75.000
CI	Very Strong	97.920	150.000	70	2000.000	75.000

☐ Assign 'C' Values   OK

The completed data form is shown below:

Pipe Material	Corrosion Index	Max. Pressure	Max. Load	Design Life	Max. Diameter	Min. Diameter
AC	Very Strong	35.700	23.500	60	2500.000	50.000
RCC	Very Strong	30.000	30.000	60	1200.000	400.000
U1	Very Strong	15.000	25.000	50	1000.000	300.000
PVC	Very Strong	15.300	4.400	60	1200.000	75.000
CI	Very Strong	97.920	150.000	70	2000.000	75.000

☐ Assign 'C' Values   OK

To define the 'Pipe Material: Age-C' relationship, the user should click on the check box 'Assign 'C' Values' on the 'Pipe Material Properties Input Form'. This opens the 'Pipe Material: Age-'C' Values Relation Input Form'. Again, if the default database for the pipe material in the IRA-WDS program contains the pipe material listed in water distribution pipe theme, 'C' values appear in the check boxes; otherwise the check boxes remain empty. (Note that values are assigned up to the designed age of the pipe and '0' 'C' values are assigned for any ages greater than the designed age of the pipe). An input form filled in with values from the database is shown below:

Pipe Material : Age - 'C' Values Relation Input Form										
Material \ Age	0 - 10 yrs	11 - 20 yrs	21 - 30 yrs	31 - 40 yrs	41 - 50 yrs	51 - 60 yrs	61 - 70 yrs	71 - 80 yrs	81 - 90 yrs	91 - 100 yrs
AC	150	130	130	120	120	120	100	0	0	0
RCC	130	120	110	95	70	70	70	0	0	0
U1										
PVC	150	140	140	140	140	140	130	0	0	0
CI	150	110	100	90	80	70	70	60	0	0

OK

The user needs to complete the form appropriately by entering values in any blank fields. He or she can also modify the data if they do not agree with the default database. The completed data form is shown below:

Pipe Material : Age - 'C' Values Relation Input Form										
Material \ Age	0 - 10 yrs	11 - 20 yrs	21 - 30 yrs	31 - 40 yrs	41 - 50 yrs	51 - 60 yrs	61 - 70 yrs	71 - 80 yrs	81 - 90 yrs	91 - 100 yrs
AC	150	130	130	120	120	120	100	0	0	0
RCC	130	120	110	95	70	70	70	0	0	0
U1	120	120	110	110	100	90	0	0	0	0
PVC	150	140	140	140	140	140	130	0	0	0
CI	150	110	100	90	80	70	70	60	0	0

OK

4.5 Other data

The remaining data used is in quantitative (crisp data) and qualitative (fuzzy data) forms, which are described below.

Crisp data

The parameters that are quantitative in nature are: 'Pipe Diameter', 'Pipe Length', 'Pipe Material', 'Pipe Age', 'Number of Connections', 'Number of Breakages', 'Pipe Buried Depth', 'Number of Valves', 'Duration of Water Supply per Day' and 'Frequency of Water Supplied per Day'. Except for the 'Pipe Age', the remainder of the parameters do not require any more information. These parameters need to be selected if required. For 'Pipe Age', further information pertaining to the 'Analysis Year' is required, which can be selected from the combo box, as shown below:

Fuzzy data

The parameters that are qualitative in nature are: the 'Pipe Material Corrosion Index', 'Pipe Internal and External Protection', 'Soil Corrosivity', 'Surface Type/Permeability', 'Ground Water Table Fluctuation', 'Traffic Density', 'Maximum Pressure', 'Pipe Joint Methods', 'Pipe Bedding Condition' and 'Workmanship'. All of these require further information regarding their membership function.

4.5.1 Membership functions

If any fuzzy parameter is clicked, its membership definition form appears. For example, if Pipe Material and then Corrosion Index Membership Function are clicked, its membership form appears (see screen below). The form is common for all the parameters except the title and group labels, which vary according to the indicator for which membership function is to be defined.

63

The form consists of five buttons and 20 text boxes for user input. The membership function is defined with the help of these text boxes. A trapezoidal or triangular membership function can be defined with this input form. If the 'Middle Left' and 'Middle Right' values of the membership form are the same, the membership function is triangular. The membership form that appears on the screen contains the default values membership function. However, the user can change the membership function. He or she is advised to refer to the Book-3 (Risk assessment of contaminant intrusion into water distribution systems) of this series for this purpose.

There are five buttons to facilitate defining membership functions. These are:

Default: Clicking this button loads the membership definition text boxes with default values defined for various indicators in the IRA-WDS database.

Clear All: Clicking this button clears all membership definition text boxes.

OK: By clicking this button, the membership definition is completed and the membership definition dialogue box is closed.

Cancel: By clicking this button the membership definition is cancelled and the dialogue box is closed.

Chart: By clicking this button, the membership definition and the 'Pipe Condition Assessment Input Form' are minimized and the layout dialogue box is opened within which the membership defined is shown graphically.

1. Pipe Material Corrosion Index

Assign Membership Function for :				
CORROSION INDEX				
	Left	Middle Left	Middle Right	Right
Very Weak	0.0	0.0	0.1	0.2
Weak	0.1	0.3	0.3	0.5
Medium	0.3	0.5	0.5	0.7
Strong	0.5	0.7	0.7	0.9
Very Strong	0.8	0.9	1.0	1.0

Default | Clear All | OK | Cancel | Chart

64

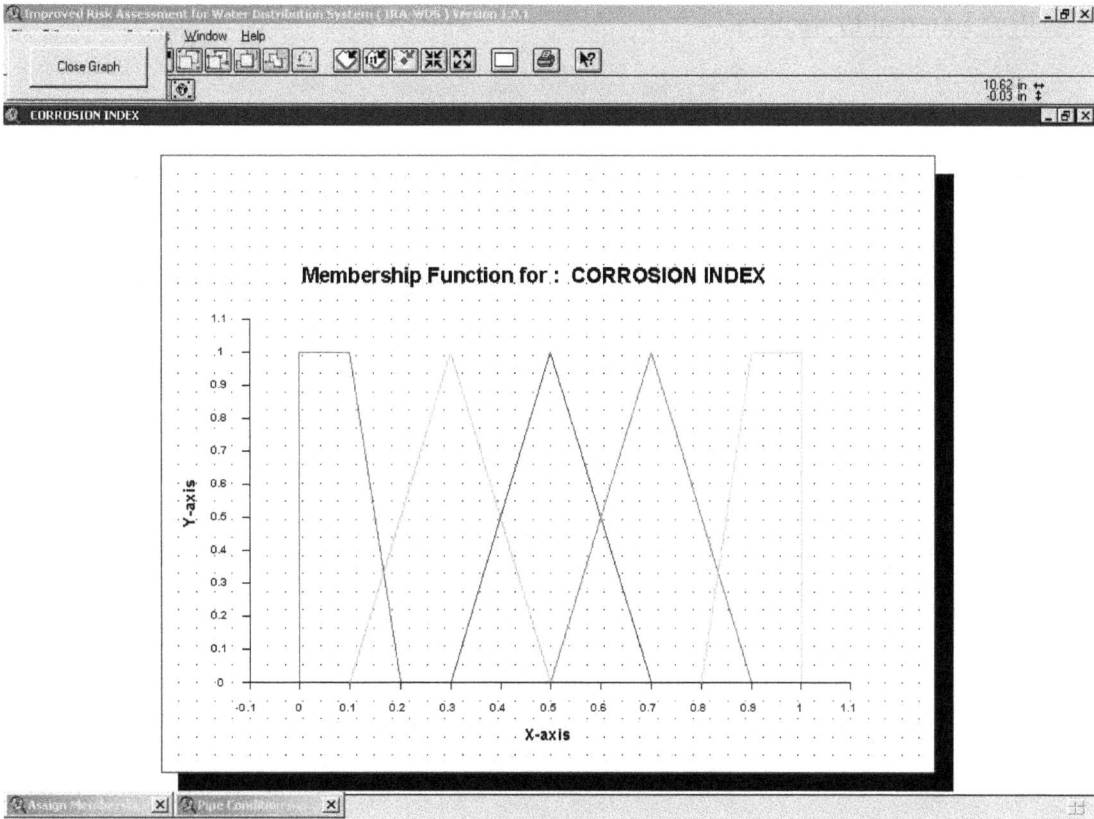

2. Pipe Internal Protection

3. Pipe External Protection

Assign Membership Function for :

EXTERNAL PROTECTION

	Left	Middle Left	Middle Right	Right
Very Bad	0.0	0.0	0.1	0.2
Bad	0.1	0.3	0.3	0.5
Medium	0.3	0.5	0.5	0.7
Good	0.5	0.7	0.7	0.9
Very Good	0.8	0.9	1.0	1.0

Default | Clear All | OK | Cancel | Chart

4. Soil Corrosivity

When defining the soil corrosivity membership function, the 'Soil Corrosivity' property is used.

Assign Membership Function for :

SOIL CORROSIVITY

	Left	Middle Left	Middle Right	Right
Non Corrosive	0.0	100.0	500.0	1000.0
Mildly Corrosiv	100.0	600.0	1000.0	2000.0
Corrosive	1000.0	1500.0	1800.0	2500.0
Highly Corrosiv	2000.0	2500.0	3000.0	5000.0
Extremely Corr	4000.0	6000.0	8000.0	20000.0

Default | Clear All | OK | Cancel | Chart

5. Surface Type/Permeability

Assign Membership Function for :

SURFACE PERMEABILITY

	Left	Middle Left	Middle Right	Right
Very Hard	0.0	0.0	0.1	0.2
Hard	0.1	0.3	0.3	0.5
Grassed	0.3	0.5	0.5	0.7
Open Land	0.5	0.7	0.7	0.9
Water Body	0.8	0.9	1.0	1.0

Default | Clear All | OK | Cancel | Chart

6. Ground Water Table Fluctuation

Assign Membership Function for :

GROUND WATER FLUCTUATION

	Left	Middle Left	Middle Right	Right
Very Bad	0.0	0.0	0.1	0.2
Bad	0.1	0.3	0.3	0.5
Medium	0.3	0.5	0.5	0.7
Good	0.5	0.7	0.7	0.9
Very Good	0.8	0.9	1.0	1.0

Default | Clear All | OK | Cancel | Chart

7. Traffic Density

When defining the traffic density membership function, the actual observed values of number of vehicles passing per hour should be used.

Assign Membership Function for :

TRAFFIC DENSITY

	Left	Middle Left	Middle Right	Right
Very Busy	45.0	50.0	60.0	80.0
Busy	35.0	40.0	45.0	50.0
Medium	25.0	30.0	35.0	40.0
Quite	10.0	20.0	25.0	30.0
Very Quite	0.0	5.0	10.0	15.0

Default | Clear All | OK | Cancel | Chart

8. Maximum Pressure

When defining the maximum pressure membership function, the values of pressure at the outlets should be used.

Assign Membership Function for :

MAXIMUM PRESSURE

	Left	Middle Left	Middle Right	Right
Very High	45.0	50.0	60.0	80.0
High	35.0	40.0	45.0	50.0
Medium	25.0	30.0	35.0	40.0
Low	10.0	20.0	25.0	30.0
Very Low	0.0	5.0	10.0	15.0

Default | Clear All | OK | Cancel | Chart

9. Joint Method

Assign Membership Function for :

JOINT METHOD

	Left	Middle Left	Middle Right	Right
Very Bad	0.0	0.0	0.1	0.2
Bad	0.1	0.4	0.4	0.7
Medium	0.4	0.65	0.65	0.9
Good	0.6	0.8	1.0	1.0
Very Good	0.8	0.9	1.0	1.0

Default | Clear All | OK | Cancel | Chart

10. Bedding Condition

Assign Membership Function for :

BEDDING CONDITION

	Left	Middle Left	Middle Right	Right
Very Bad	0.0	0.0	0.1	0.2
Bad	0.1	0.3	0.3	0.5
Medium	0.3	0.5	0.5	0.7
Good	0.5	0.7	0.7	0.9
Very Good	0.8	0.9	1.0	1.0

Default | Clear All | OK | Cancel | Chart

11. Workmanship

Assign Membership Function for :

WORKMANSHIP

	Left	Middle Left	Middle Right	Right
Very Bad	0.0	0.0	0.1	0.2
Bad	0.1	0.3	0.3	0.5
Medium	0.3	0.5	0.5	0.7
Good	0.5	0.7	0.7	0.9
Very Good	0.8	0.9	1.0	1.0

Default | Clear All | OK | Cancel | Chart

4.5.2 Weightage methods

The user also needs to assign weights for various indicators and balance factors for various groups. Weight allows importance to be given to different parameters/indicators within a group. Balance factors reflect the importance of the maximal deviations between indicators (criteria) in the same group, where 'maximal deviation' means the maximum difference between an indicator value and the best value for that indicator. The larger the balancing factor, the greater the concern with respect to the maximal deviation. Low balancing factors are used for a high level of allowable compromise between indicators of the same group. A balancing factor equal to 1 means that there is a perfect compromise between indicators of the group. If the level of compromise between indicators is moderate, a balancing factor of 2 will be sufficient. A balancing factor of 3 or more reflects a situation of minimal compromise between indicators. In the present (Pipe Condition Assessment) model, three weightage methods are included. These are:

Equal Weights: With this method, equal weights are assigned to all the indicators of particular group. A balancing factor of 1 is assigned to all the groups.

Assign Weights: With this method, weights are assigned directly. The form in which they are assigned is shown below:

Assign Weights for Pipe Condition Assessment

Pipe Condition Assessment

Physical Indicators

Pipe Indicators		Installation Indicators	
Diameter	0.200	Joint Method	0.250
Length	0.200	Bed. Condition	0.250
Material	0.200	Workmanship	0.250
Int. Protect.	0.200		
Ext. Protect.	0.200	Connections	0.250
Balance Factor		Balance Factor	

Environmental Indicators

Corrosion Indicators		Strength Indicators	
Pipe Age	0.250	Burried Depth	0.333
Soil Corrosivity	0.250	Traffic Density	0.333
Surface Type	0.250		
Groundwater	0.250	Pressure	0.333
Balance Factor		Balance Factor	

Operational Indicators

Failure Indicators		Intermittancy Indicators	
		Valve Number	0.333
Breakage	1.000	Operation Time	0.333
		No. of Operations	0.333
Balance Factor		Balance Factor	

Pipe Weight	0.5	Corrosion Weight	0.5
Installation Weight	0.5	Strength Weight	0.5
Physical Balance Factor		Environmental Balance Factor	
Failure Weight	0.5		
Intermittancy Weight	0.5		
Operational Balance Factor			

Physical Weight	0.333
Environmental Weight	0.333
Operational Weight	0.333
Pipe Condition Assessment Balance Factor	

Assign Weights   Cancel

Depending on the number of indicators selected for the assessment, equal weights are assigned initially to all the indicators. The user can change the weights assigned to each indicator. However, it is necessary that the sum of the weights given in one group should be equal to 1 (see screen above). The user needs to input values for the balance factors of each group. After completing the form, the user can click on the 'Assign Weights' button to assign the weights and close the form. The program then displays the following Information message regarding weights assigned. Clicking on 'OK' closes this form.

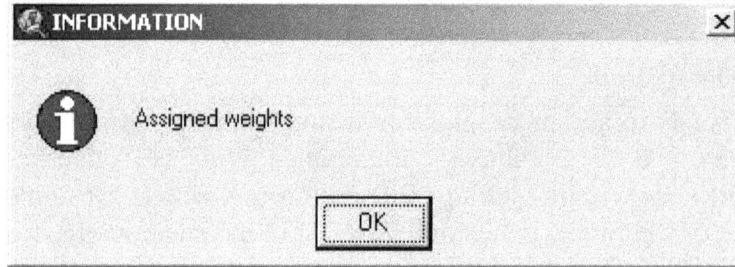

Generated by AHP: Weights can also be generated using the pair-wise comparison, that is, by Analytical Hierarchy Process (AHP). Clicking on 'Generate Weights' causes the following 'Generate Weights using Analytical Hierarchy Process' form to appear.

The matrix elements are enabled for those indicators that are selected in the 'Pipe Condition Assessment Input Form'. The slider on the right-hand side of the 'Generate Weightings using Analytical Hierarchy Process' form can be used to define the matrix element. The user needs to input values for the balance factors of each group. On completion of the matrix elements and inputting the balance factors, the form appears as shown in the example in next page.

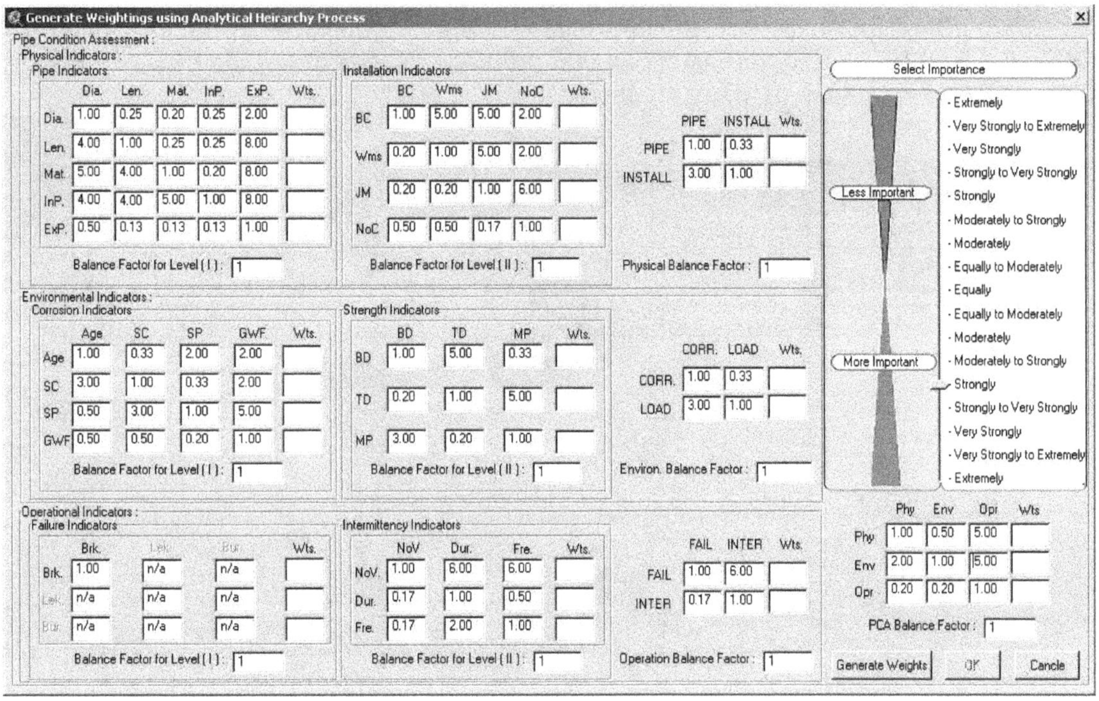

The user then clicks the 'Generate Weights' button, which opens the 'Save AHP Input File' dialogue box to save the AHP input matrix, as shown below:

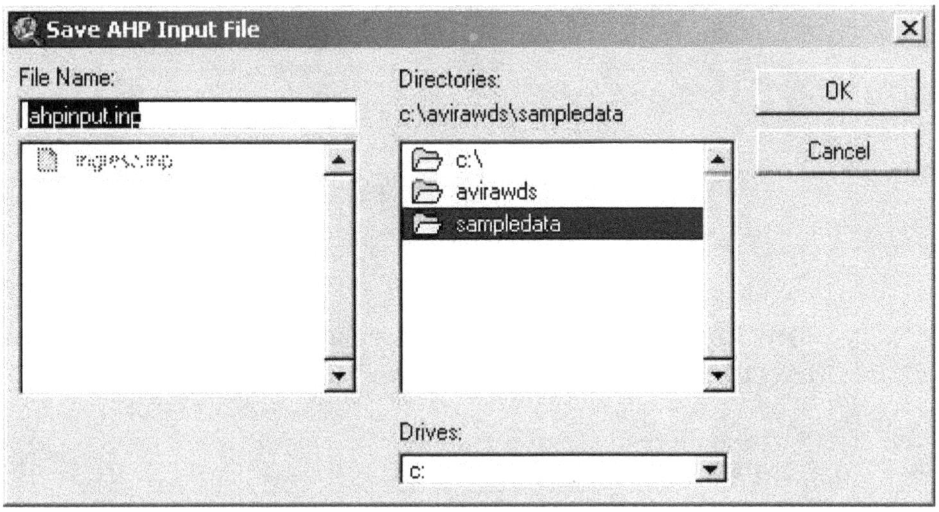

After selecting the input filename to save AHP input, the following dialogue box appears:

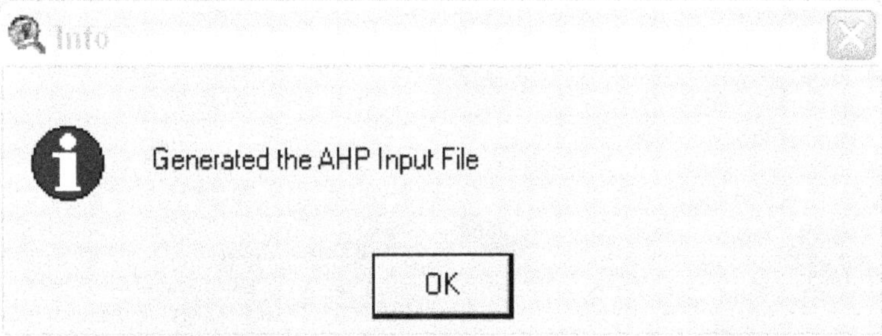

Confirming 'OK' on the 'Generated the AHP Input File' Info message box opens the 'Save AHP Output File' dialogue box and prompts the user about the filename to save the AHP output under, as shown below:

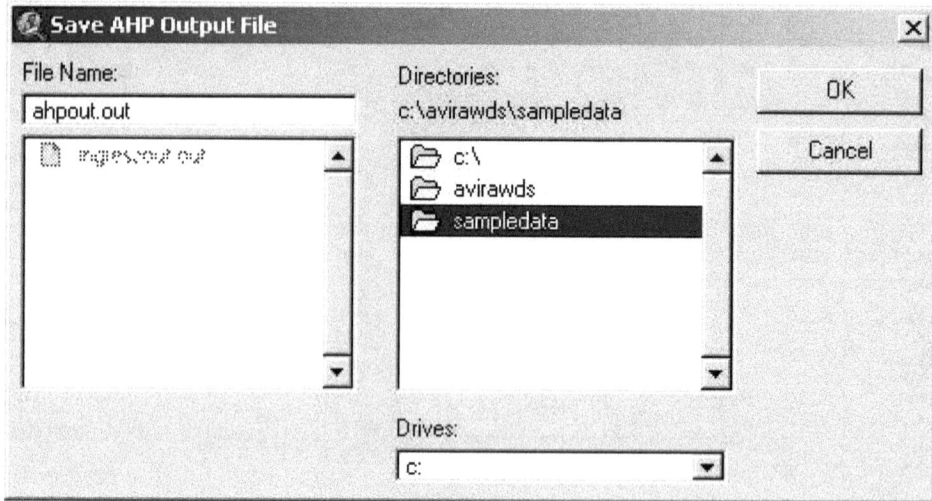

After selecting the output filename to save AHP output under, the following dialogue box appears:

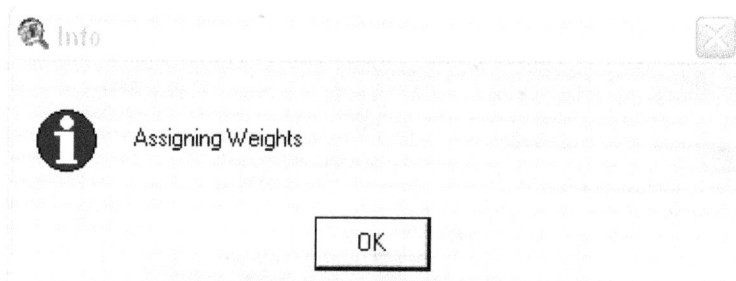

Clicking 'OK' executes the AHP model, which generates the weight for each parameter considered in the 'Pipe Condition Assessment Input Form' and then asks the name of AHP output file for viewing, as shown below:

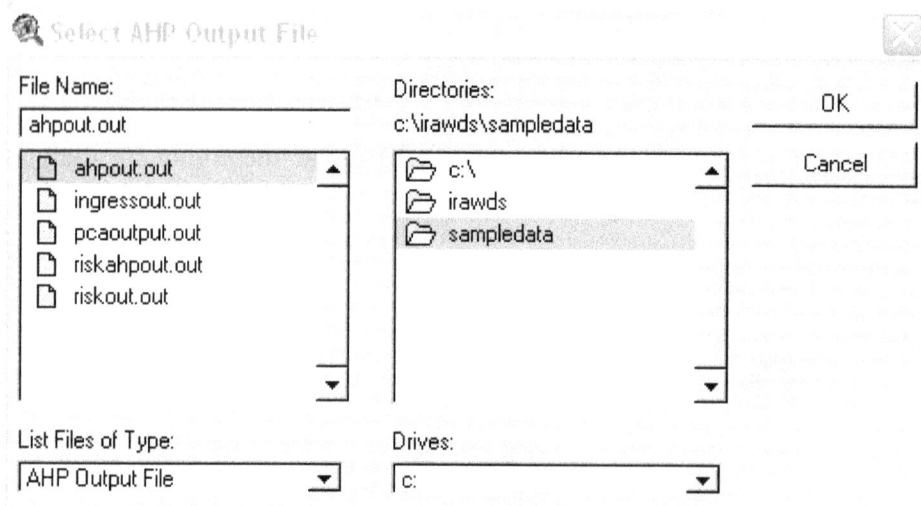

After the user gives the name of AHP output file, the following message appears:

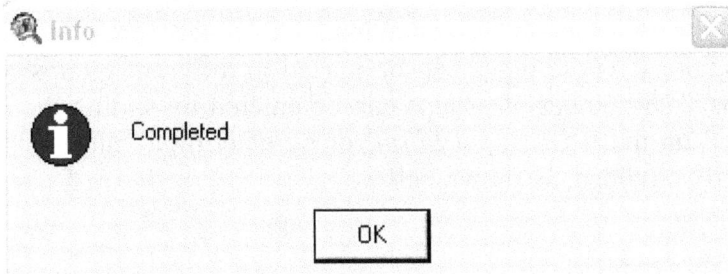

After the user confirms 'OK', the weights can be seen (see screen below). If the weights generated using AHP are consistent, then those values are presented in the respective text boxes; otherwise '–99' appears in those boxes. If any particular indicator is not considered in the analysis, then '–999' appears in the text box as shown below:

During this step the 'Generate Weights' button is disabled and 'OK' button is enabled. If the user clicks the 'OK' button, then the weights generated by AHP are assigned and a message is displayed as shown below:

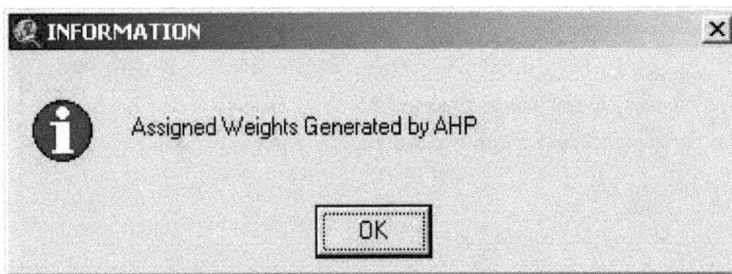

If the 'Cancel' button is clicked, then the 'Equal Weights' option will be selected and 'Weights by AHP' will not be selected.

4.6 Number of groups

The output of the PCA model is a ranking of different pipes depending on their respective conditions. These pipes can be placed in different groups on the basis of their conditions. The number of groups can be entered by sliding the bar in front of 'No. of Groups' on the 'PCA Input Form' or by entering a value for the number of groups in the box provided, as shown below:

4.7 Generating the input file (PCA)

To generate the pipe condition assessment input file, the user should click on the 'Generate Input' button on the 'Pipe Condition Assessment Input Form'. If 'Soil Corrosivity' is selected, the model finds which pipe falls in which soil type and then appends the water distribution system pipe theme with soil corrosion category data accordingly.

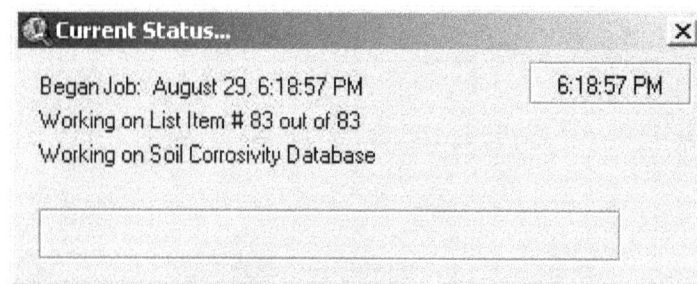

If the 'Ground Water Table' is selected, the interface finds the average groundwater table depth and groundwater fluctuation depth for each pipe. Then using the pipe buried depth and the groundwater table data, it computes the groundwater category for each pipe and appends the water distribution pipe theme accordingly.

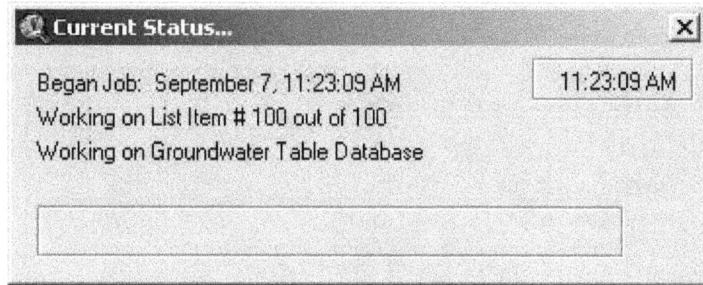

If the 'Maximum Pressure' is selected, the interface finds the pressure for each pipe and then appends the water distribution pipe theme according to the pressure category.

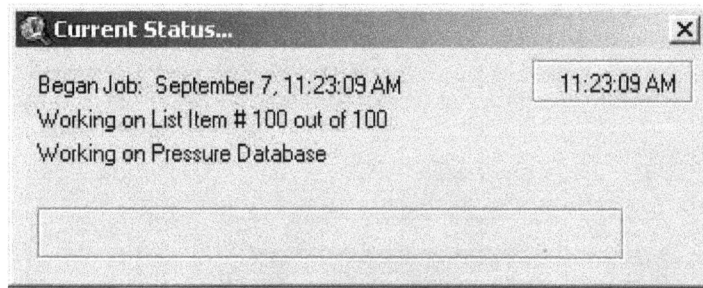

It then opens the 'File Save' dialogue box to save the file with the user-defined name.

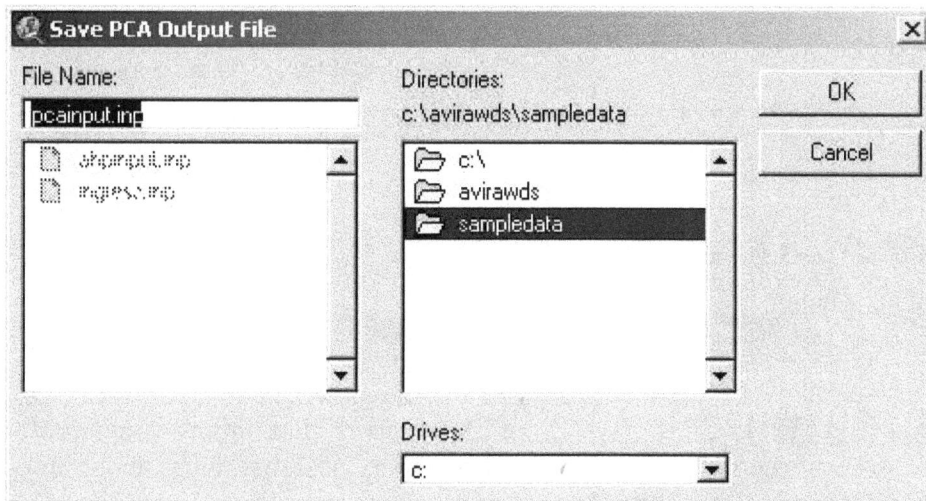

After the user writes/selects the input filename, the interface starts writing the input file. The data generation and writing progress is shown in the 'Current Status...' bar, as shown below:

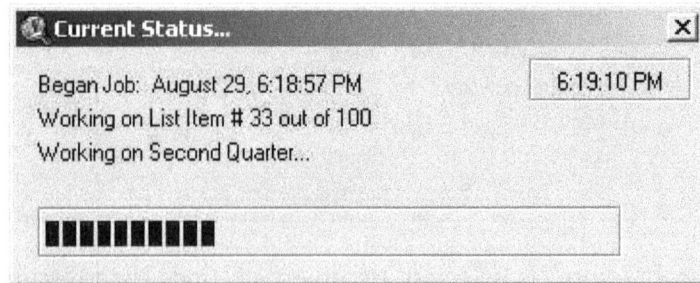

Before completion of data writing, the model prompts an 'Input Choice' box asking the user for a 'Local Analysis' or 'Global Analysis' of pipe condition.

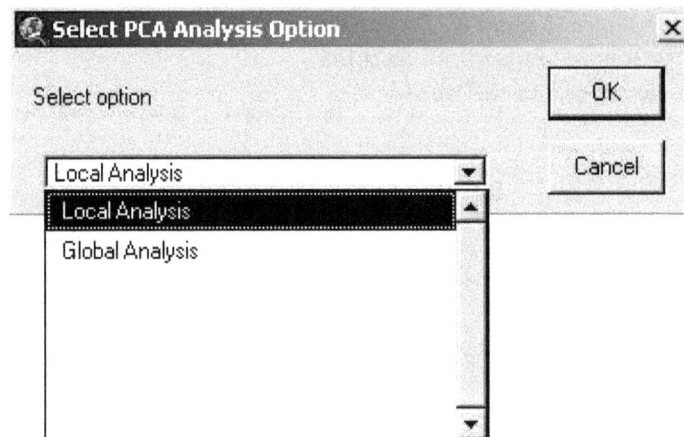

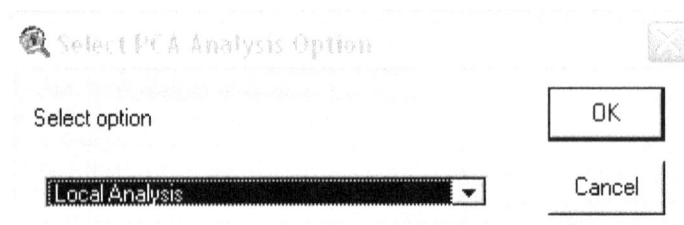

If user selects the 'Local Analysis' option, no more data input is required and the interface scans through the data input and finds the local maximum and minimum for the particular parameter required.

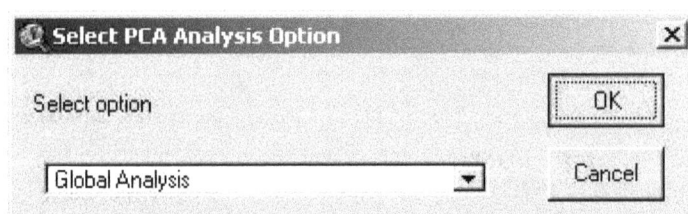

If the 'Global Analysis' option is selected, then one more input form is opened asking the user to fill in the maximum and minimum for certain parameters; these can then be used to study and compare different networks in different conditions. The 'Global Data' input form is shown below:

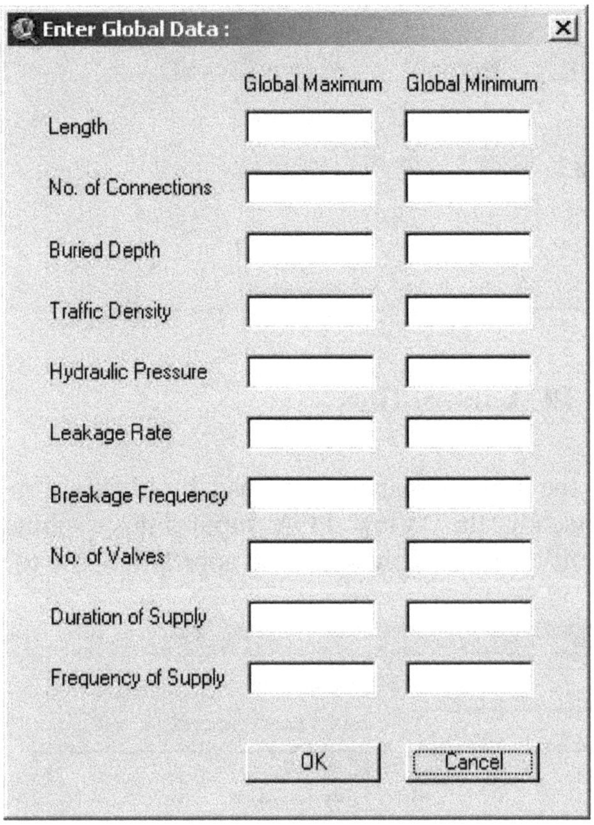

After the user has completed the data, the 'Global Data' input form looks as shown below:

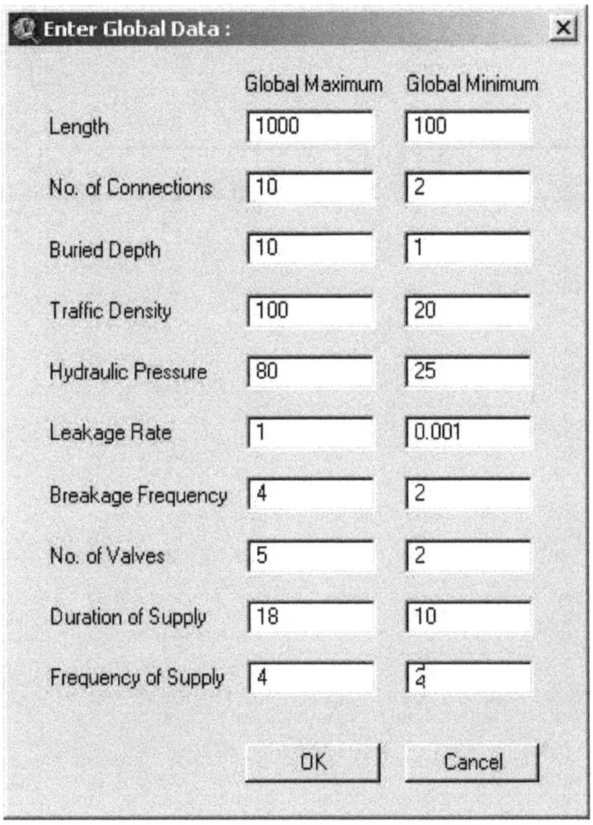

After completing the data, the user can click on the 'OK' button. After generating the input file successfully, an 'Info' message box indicating 'Input File Generation completion' is displayed as shown below:

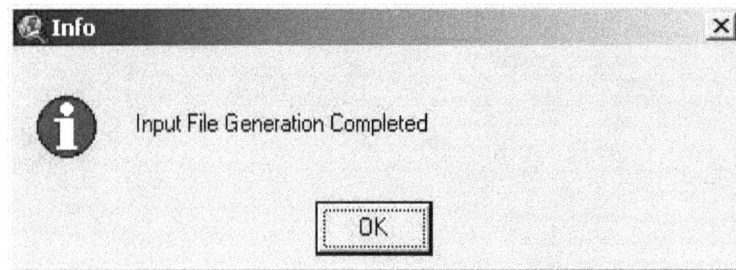

4.8 Viewing the PCA input files

The user can view the input file in the notepad by clicking on the [T] button or alternatively by selecting the 'View PCA Input Files' submenu from the 'Pipe Condition Assessment' menu and browsing the appropriate file to view.

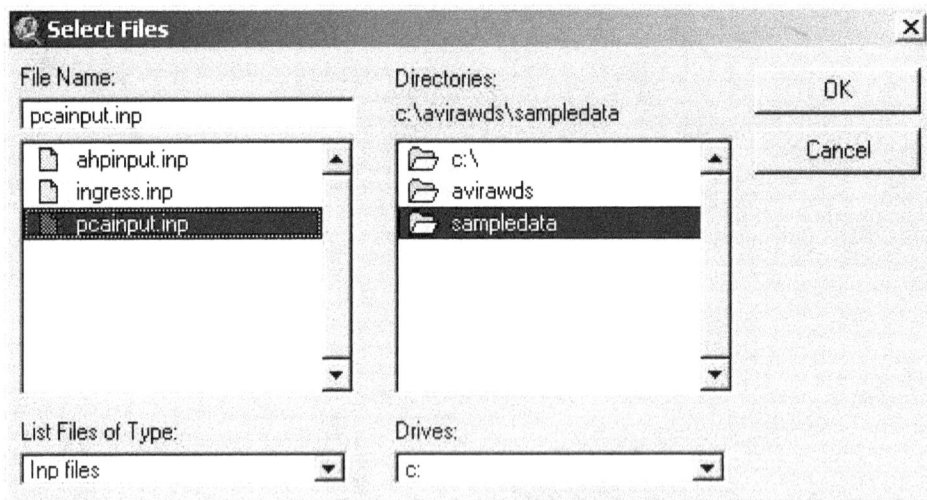

```
pcainput - Notepad
File Edit Format Help
;==========================================;
;      WATER PIPELINE Vulnerability Assessment Input
;==========================================;

[WATER PIPE]
;ID    StNode EndNode StJoint EndJoint    Material    Traffic SurfPerm    InProtect    ExProtect    BedCond Workship

689  631  632  4  4  0  2  0  2  1  0  4  0  1  2  500  50 120  1.312
703  632  643  1  1  0  2  2  2  4  4  1  0  1  2  500  50 120  51.20
722  660  631  1  1  1  2  2  2  4  3  1  0  1  2  500  50 70  21.79
762  643  696  2  2  0  2  2  2  4  3  2  0  1  2  400  50 120  48.79
781  696  713  2  2  0  2  2  2  4  3  3  0  1  2  400  50 120  13.70
786  719  660  2  2  1  2  2  2  4  4  2  0  1  2  500  50 70  57.72
796  713  728  2  2  0  2  2  2  4  3  2  0  1  2  400  50 120  65.78
800  732  719  2  2  0  3  2  2  4  1  2  0  1  2  500  50 70  17.32
803  734  732  2  2  1  3  2  2  4  1  2  0  1  2  500  50 70  1.848
808  728  739  2  2  0  2  0  2  1  3  3  1  1  1  400  35 120  37.87
809  740  734  2  2  1  3  2  2  4  1  2  0  1  2  500  50 70  18.99
818  739  747  2  2  0  2  0  2  1  3  3  1  1  1  400  35 120  62.12
824  753  740  2  2  1  3  2  2  4  1  3  1  1  1  200  50 70  72.37
830  747  758  2  2  0  3  0  2  1  3  4  1  1  1  400  35 120  48.64
831  760  753  2  2  1  3  0  2  1  3  2  0  1  2  200  50 70  27.62
836  765  728  2  2  0  2  0  2  1  3  3  1  1  2  400  20 130  38.94
837  765  760  2  2  1  2  0  2  1  3  2  1  1  2  400  20 120  25.67
842  758  769  2  2  0  2  0  2  1  3  4  1  4  1  400  35 120  38.08
852  777  765  2  2  1  3  0  2  1  1  2  1  1  1  200  35 95  37.53
855  780  765  2  2  0  3  0  2  1  1  2  1  1  2  200  20 130  12.74
856  781  734  2  2  2  4  2  1  4  1  2  0  1  2  500  50 100  61.00
861  785  781  2  2  2  4  2  1  4  1  2  0  1  2  200  20 120  3.559
862  786  785  2  2  2  4  2  1  4  1  2  0  1  2  200  20 120  0.308
865  769  788  1  1  0  3  0  2  1  3  4  1  4  1  400  35 120  54.68
866  789  777  2  2  2  3  0  2  1  1  3  1  1  2  200  35 95  40.72
879  800  786  1  1  2  3  0  2  1  1  3  0  1  1  200  20 120  19.12
880  789  801  2  2  1  3  0  2  1  1  2  1  1  2  200  35 95  36.71
883  801  806  2  2  1  3  0  2  1  1  4  1  4  1  400  35 95  36.38
884  807  758  2  2  1  2  0  2  1  3  4  1  4  1  400  35 95  37.14
885  806  807  2  2  1  3  0  2  1  1  4  1  4  1  200  35 95  0.517
892  814  785  1  1  2  4  2  1  4  1  2  0  1  2  200  20 120  30.13
893  815  814  1  1  2  4  2  1  4  1  2  0  1  2  200  20 120  3.216
898  807  821  2  2  1  3  0  2  1  1  4  1  4  1  200  35 95  37.69
899  821  822  2  2  1  3  0  2  1  1  4  1  1  2  200  35 95  1.133
900  823  815  1  1  2  4  2  1  4  1  2  0  1  2  200  20 120  11.45
905  827  800  1  1  2  4  2  1  4  1  2  0  1  2  200  20 120  35.15
914  834  788  1  1  0  3  0  2  1  3  4  1  4  1  400  35 120  35.88
915  822  834  1  1  1  3  0  2  1  1  4  1  4  1  200  35 95  52.62
917  815  836  1  1  2  4  2  1  4  1  2  0  1  2  200  20 120  30.48
918  801  837  2  2  0  1  0  2  1  1  3  1  4  1  200  35 120  31.21
920  839  834  1  1  0  3  0  2  1  1  4  1  1  2  200  35 120  7.589
936  852  827  1  1  0  1  0  1  1  1  4  1  1  2  200  20 120  64.84
942  858  839  1  1  0  3  0  2  1  1  4  1  4  1  200  35 120  17.21
944  760  860  2  2  0  1  0  2  1  1  2  1  1  2  200  20 130  85.53
945  852  860  2  2  0  1  0  2  1  1  2  0  1  2  200  20 120  33.33
949  836  863  1  1  2  4  2  1  4  1  2  0  1  2  200  20 130  69.51
950  865  780  2  2  0  1  0  2  1  1  2  1  1  2  200  20 130  74.34
951  860  865  2  2  0  1  0  2  1  1  2  2  1  2  200  20 130  25.65
956  869  852  1  1  2  1  0  1  1  1  2  0  1  2  200  20 120  24.21
957  863  869  1  1  0  3  0  1  1  1  1  2  1  2  200  20 120  35.20
```

```
pcainput - Notepad
File Edit Format Help
1196  1039  1075  4  4  4  4  3  3  3  2  3  3  4  3  300  20 110  36.67
1220  1075  1095  4  4  4  4  3  3  3  2  3  3  4  3  300  20 110  26.47
1235  1095  1109  4  4  4  4  3  3  3  2  3  3  4  3  300  20 110  27.57
1269  1137  1109  4  4  4  4  3  3  3  2  3  3  4  3  300  20 110  44.32

[PIPE MATERIAL]
;0= AC
;1= RCC
;2= U1
;3= PVC
;4= CI
;------------------------------------------------------------
;ID    CorrResis    MaxPres    MaxLoad    MaxDia    MinDia    MaxLife
;ID    Corros  Max P    Max L    Design Life    Max CFactor    Min Cfactor    Max D    Min D
;------------------------------------------------------------
0    4    35.700    23.500    60    150    100    2500.000    50.000
1    4    30.000    30.000    60    130    70    1200.000    400.000
2    4    15.000    25.000    50    120    90    1000.000    300.000
3    4    15.300    4.400    60    150    130    1200.000    75.000
4    4    97.920    150.000    70    150    60    2000.000    75.000

[CORROSION RESISTANCE]
;0=Very Weak
;1=Weak
;2=Medium
;3=Strong
;4=Very Strong
;------------------------------------------------------------
;ID    Left    MidLeft    MidRight    Right
;------------------------------------------------------------
0    0.0    0.0    0.1    0.2
1    0.1    0.3    0.3    0.5
2    0.3    0.5    0.5    0.7
3    0.5    0.7    0.7    0.9
4    0.8    0.9    1.0    1.0

[INTER PROTECTION]
;0=Very Bad
;1=Bad
;2=Medium
;3=Good
;4=Very Good
;------------------------------------------------------------
;ID    Left    MidLeft    MidRight    Right
;------------------------------------------------------------
0    0.0    0.0    0.1    0.2
1    0.1    0.3    0.3    0.5
2    0.3    0.5    0.5    0.7
3    0.5    0.7    0.7    0.9
4    0.8    0.9    1.0    1.0

[EXTER PROTECTION]
;0=Very Bad
;1=Bad
;2=Medium
;3=Good
;4=Very Good
;------------------------------------------------------------
;ID    Left    MidLeft    MidRight    Right
```

```
26    0.352189
27    0.559065
28    0.559065

[BALANCE FACTOR]
;0=Pipe Members Balance Factor;
;1=Installation Members Balance Factor;
;2=Corrosion Members Balance Factor;
;3=Strength Members Balance Factor;
;4=Failure Members Balance Factor;
;5=Intermittancy Members Balance Factor;
;6=Physical Members Balance Factor;
;7=Environmental Members Balance Factor;
;8=Operational Members Balance Factor;
;9=PCA Members Balance Factor;
;------------------------------------
;ID      balance factor
;------------------------------------
0    1
1    1
2    1
3    1
4    1
5    1
6    1
7    1
8    1
9    1

[DATA BASE]
;0=Length;
;1=No. of connections;
;2=Buried depth;
;3=Traffic load;
;4=Hydraulic pressure;
;5=Leakage frequency;
;6=Breakage frequency;
;7=Valve operation;
;8=Duration of water supply;
;9=No of water supply operation;
;------------------------------------------------
;ID     Max     Min
;------------------------------------------------
0    1000    0.308
1    10      2
2    10      1
3    100     0
4    80      0
5    1       0
6    5       0
7    5       0
8    18      2
9    4       2

[GROUP]
7

[END]
```

4.9 Loading the input file

The input file to be used for running the Pipe Condition Assessment Model is loaded using the tool [L], which is just below the 'Pipe Condition Assessment' menu or by clicking on the 'Pipe Condition Assessment' menu and then clicking on the submenu 'Load Input File', as shown in the screen below:

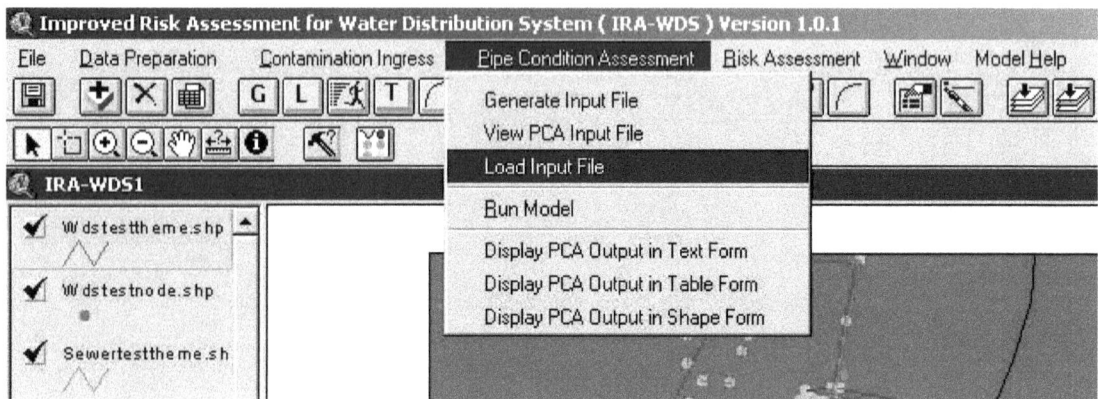

Improved Risk Assessment for Water Distribution System (IRA-WDS) Version 1.0.1

File   Data Preparation   Contamination Ingress   Pipe Condition Assessment   Risk Assessment   Window   Model Help

Generate Input File
View PCA Input File
Load Input File
Run Model

Display PCA Output in Text Form
Display PCA Output in Table Form
Display PCA Output in Shape Form

IRA-WDS1

Wdstesttheme.shp
Wdstestnode.shp
Sewertesttheme.sh

The 'Load Pipe Condition Assessment Input File' is shown below:

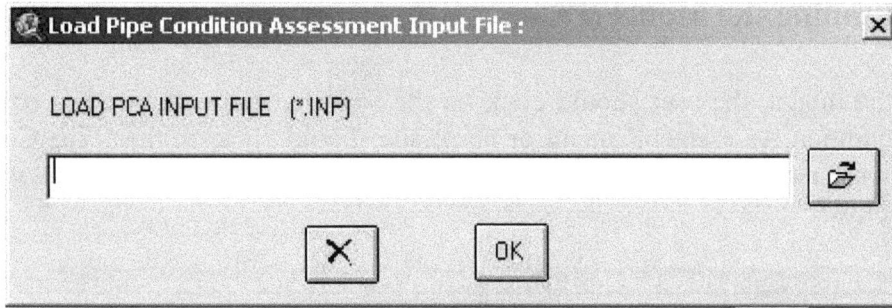

The user can browse through the computer by clicking on the ⬀ button on the 'Load Pipe Condition Assessment Input File' dialogue box. This opens the ' load files' dialogue box, as shown below:

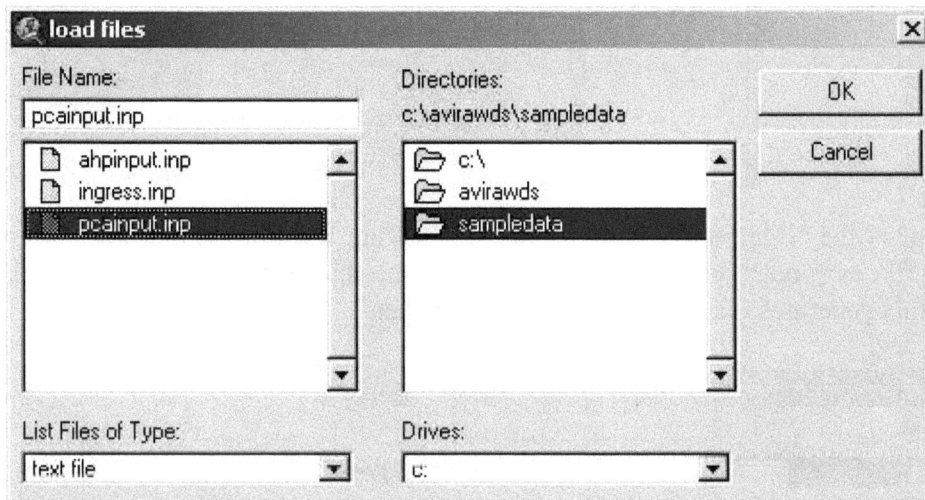

After the appropriate file has been selected and the user has pressed the 'OK' button on the filename, the filename appears in the 'Load Pipe Condition Assessment Input File' dialogue box.

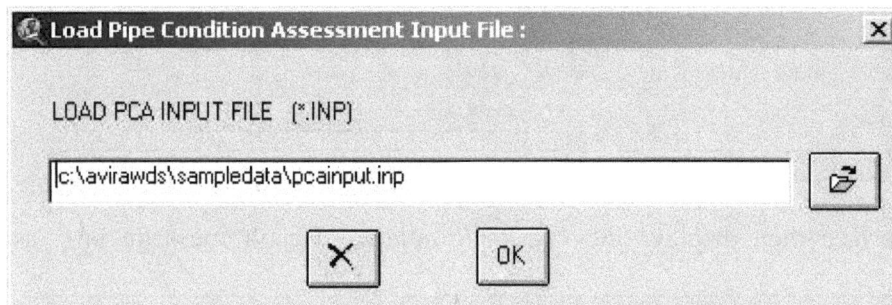

If the user wants to change the filename, he or she can do so by clicking the button ☒, which clears the filename from the 'Load Pipe Condition Assessment Input File' dialogue box. If user is sure of the input file selected, he or she can load it by clicking on the OK button. This also closes 'Load Pipe Condition Assessment Input File' dialogue box.

4.10 Running the Model (PCA)

To run the model, the user should click on the [icon] button, which is just below the 'Pipe Condition Assessment' menu or he or she should click on the 'Pipe Condition Assessment' menu and then click on the submenu 'Run Model', as shown on the screen below:

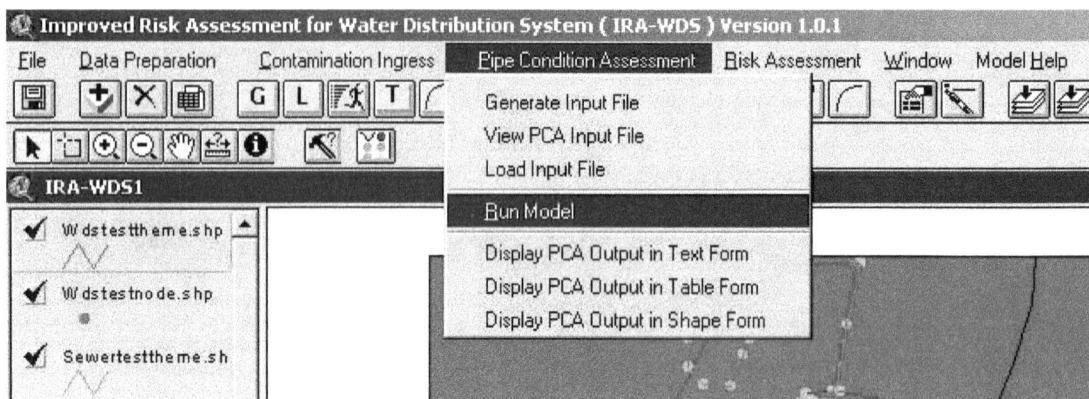

This opens the 'File Save' dialogue box for saving the Pipe Condition Assessment output file as *.out. Once the user has typed the appropriate name and clicked on 'OK', this generates the output selected by the user.

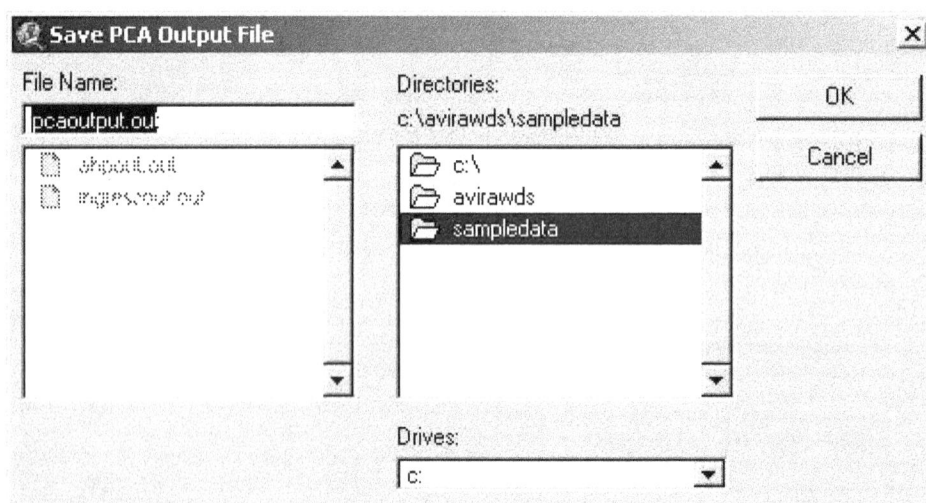

The interface then displays the 'Task Completed' Result message box, as shown below:

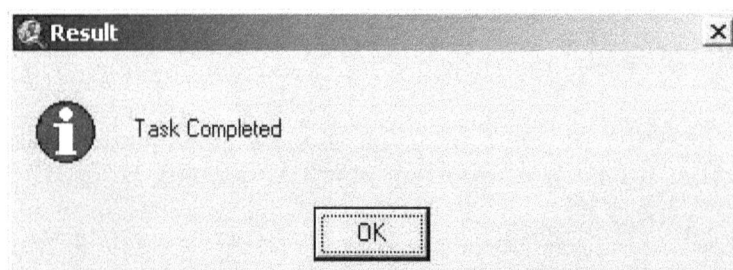

4.11 Displaying the output

Output can be displayed in the following three forms:

1. Display PCA Output in Text form
2. Display PCA Output in Table form
3. Display PCA Output in Shape form

4.11.1 Displaying PCA output in text form

The user can view the output file in the text form in notepad by clicking on the [T] button or by selecting the 'Display PCA Output in Text Form' submenu from the 'Pipe Condition Assessment' menu and browsing the appropriate output file to view.

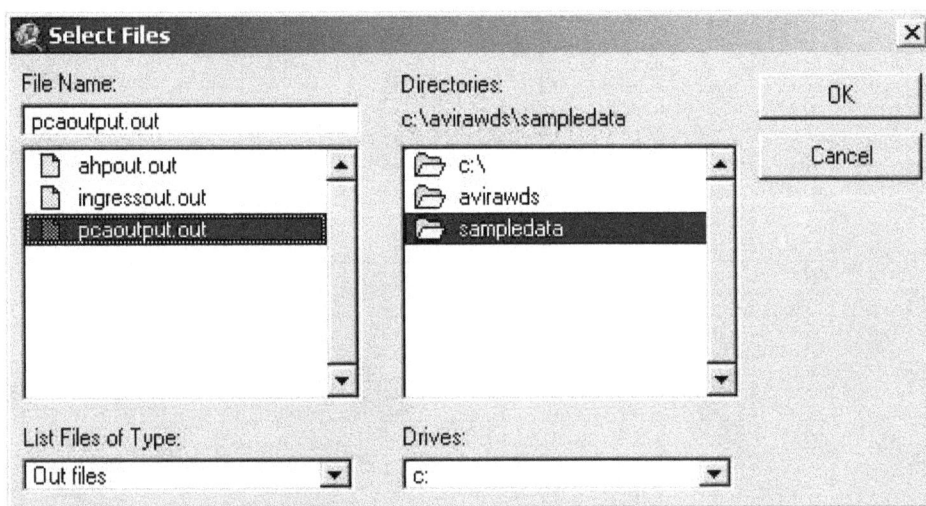

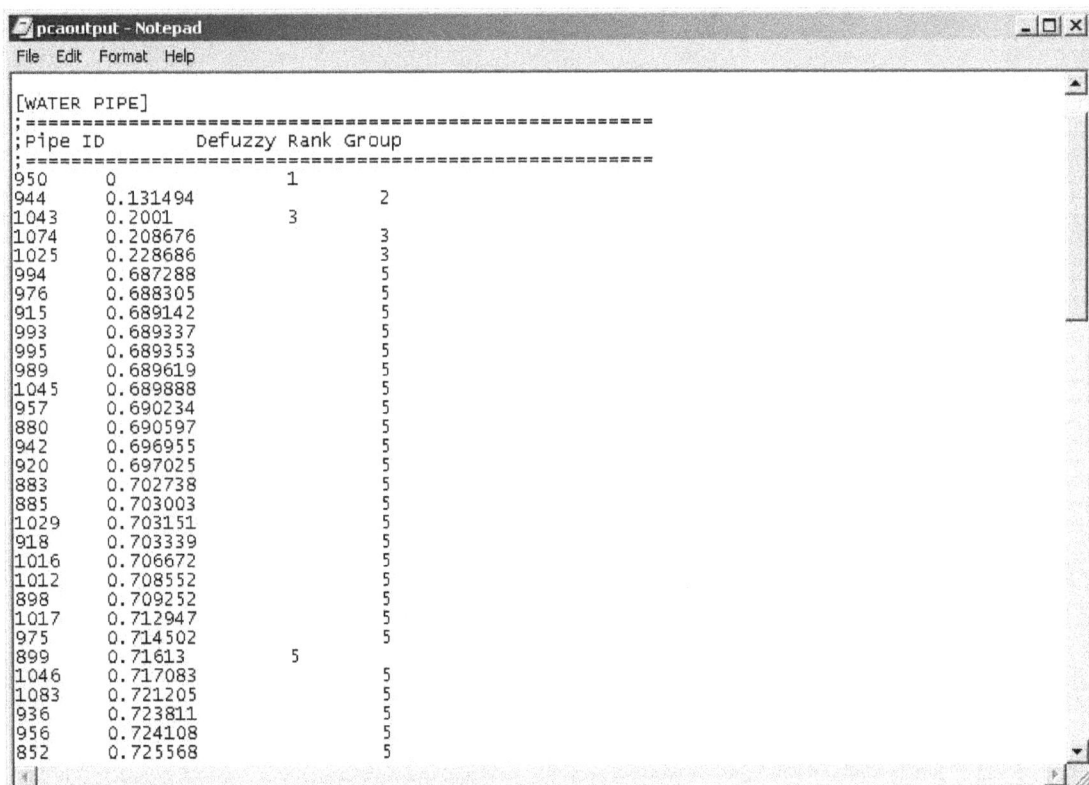

4.11.2 Displaying PCA output in table form

The user can view the output file in table form by selecting the 'Display PCA Output in Table Form' submenu from the 'Pipe Condition Assessment' menu and specifying the appropriate output file to view by browsing, as shown below:

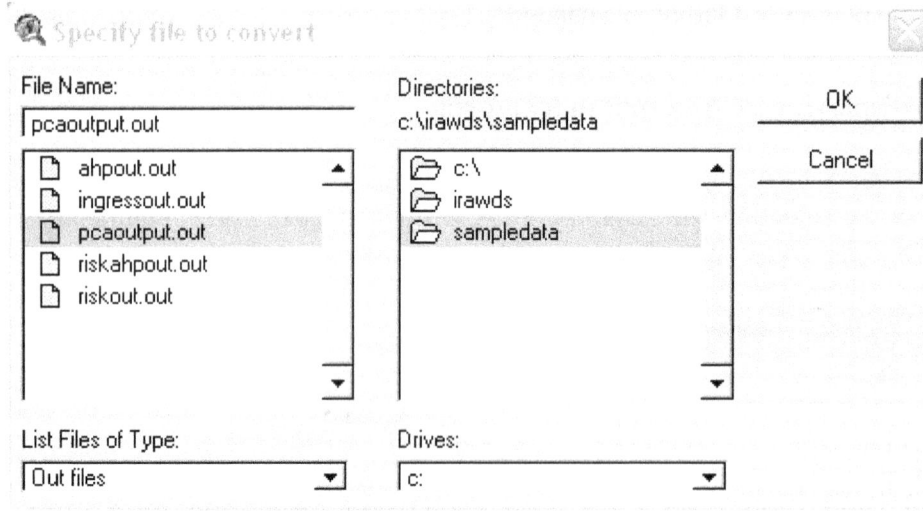

Specify file to convert

File Name:
`pcaoutput.out`

- ahpout.out
- ingressout.out
- pcaoutput.out
- riskahpout.out
- riskout.out

Directories:
`c:\irawds\sampledata`

- c:\
- irawds
- sampledata

OK

Cancel

List Files of Type:
Out files

Drives:
c:

c:\irawds\sampledata\pcaoutput.dbf

PipeID	DeFuzzy	Rank
950	0.000	1
944	0.283	3
1043	0.430	4
1074	0.448	4
1025	0.491	5
831	0.776	7
975	0.777	7
824	0.778	7
880	0.781	7
852	0.793	7
866	0.797	7
837	0.797	7
951	0.797	7
936	0.799	7
1083	0.799	7
957	0.800	8
809	0.802	8
989	0.804	8
883	0.805	8
994	0.805	8
945	0.806	8
956	0.806	8
915	0.808	8
786	0.809	8
885	0.811	8
1017	0.814	8
949	0.814	8
855	0.815	8
976	0.817	8
856	0.817	8
993	0.817	8

4.11.3 Displaying Pipe Condition Assessment output in shape form

To view the Pipe Condition Assessment output in shape file form, the user should click on the ⬜ button, which is just below the 'Pipe Condition Assessment' menu or he or she can click on the 'Pipe Condition Assessment' menu and then click on the submenu 'Display Ingress Output in Shape Form', as shown on the screen below:

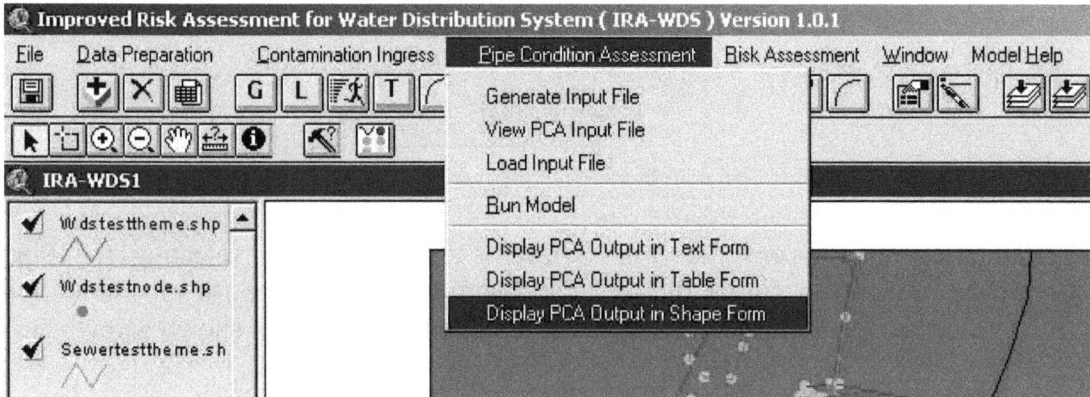

This opens the 'Display Theme' message box asking the user to specify which theme represents the water distribution system pipe theme, as shown below:

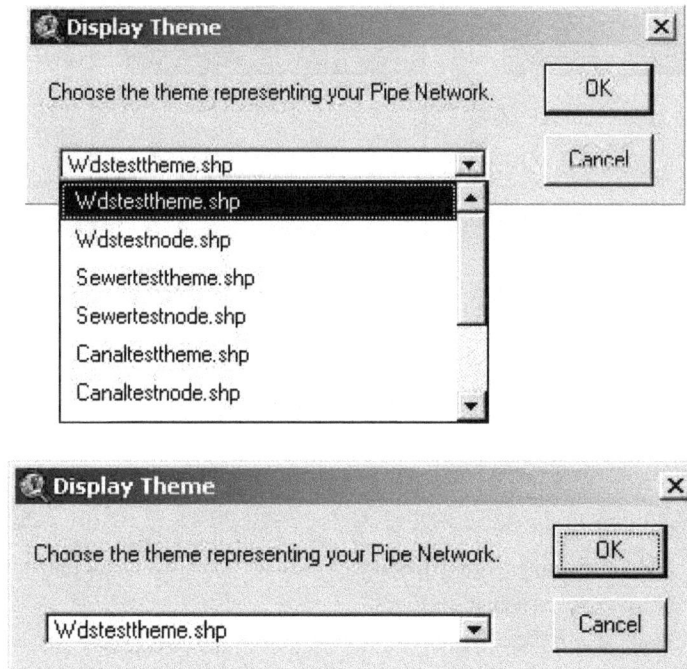

Once the user selects the appropriate theme representing the water distribution system pipe network and clicks on the 'OK' button, the 'Convert Theme' dialogue box appears on the screen and asks the user to give the name with which he or she wants to store/convert the selected theme, as shown on next page.

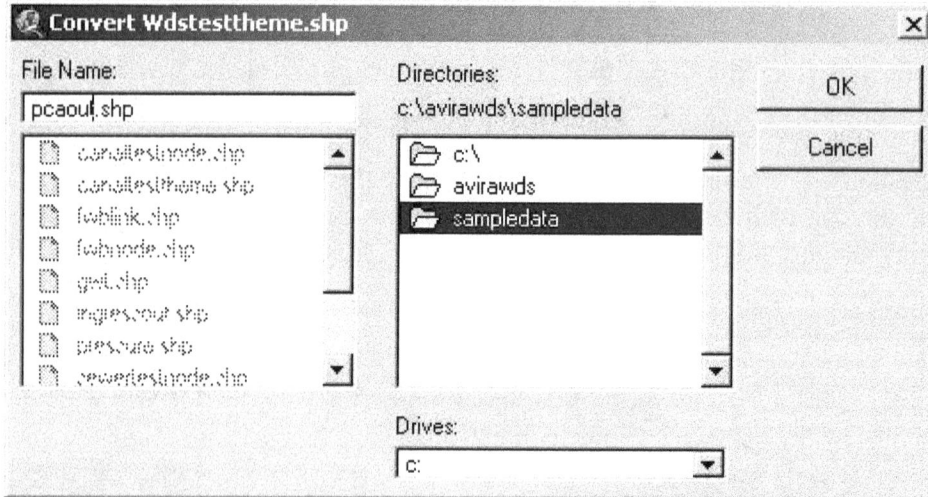

The interface then opens the 'File Select' dialogue box for selecting the Pipe Condition Assessment output file as *.out, from which attributes for pipe condition (PCAValue and PCARank) are to be added to the output theme, as shown below:

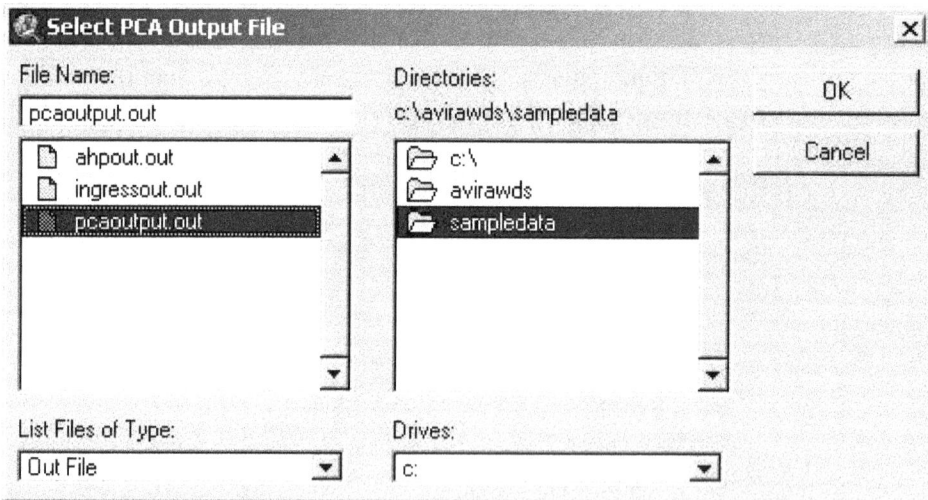

Once the user has selected the appropriate filename and clicked 'OK', the program shows the progress meter, as below:

On completion of theme generation and attribute addition, it displays the 'Completed' Info message box, as shown on next page.

After clicking the 'OK' button on this message box, the new shape-file is added to the IRA-WDS data viewer. The 'PCAOut' theme legend needs to be changed by the user and instead of viewing the theme in a single colour, it can be viewed by unique values of 'PCARank', as shown below:

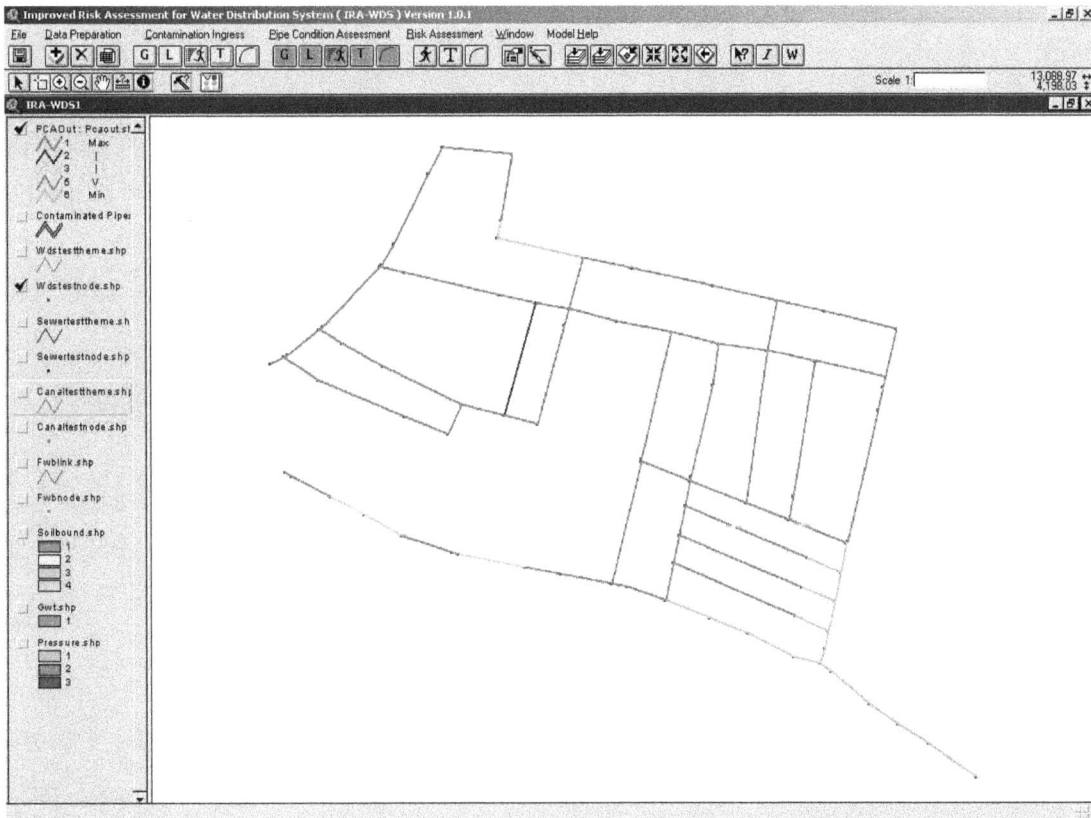

CHAPTER FIVE

Risk Assessment Model

Manual of Risk Assessment for Contaminant Intrusion into Water Distribution Systems

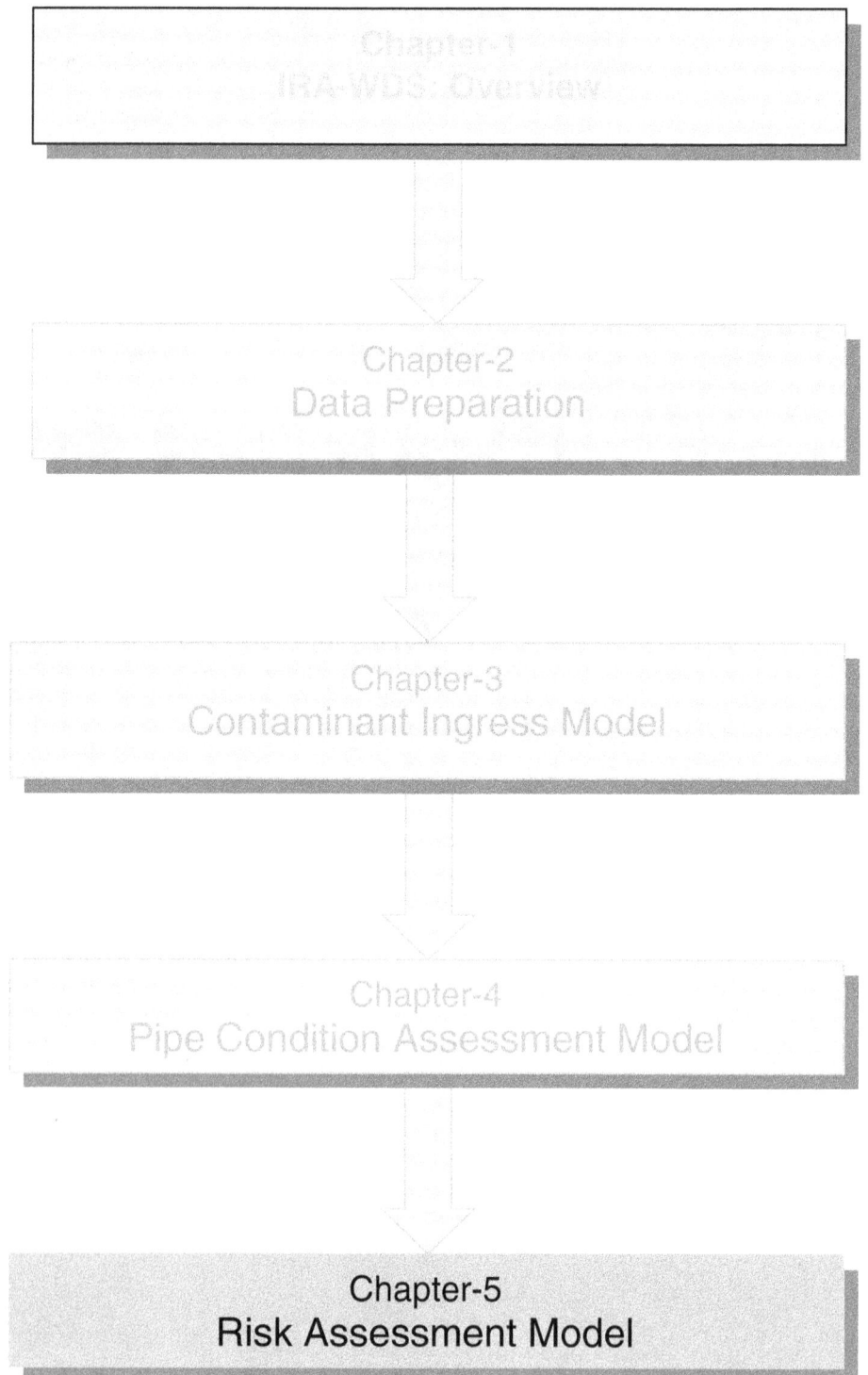

Chapter-1
IRA-WDS: Overview

Chapter-2
Data Preparation

Chapter-3
Contaminant Ingress Model

Chapter-4
Pipe Condition Assessment Model

Chapter-5
Risk Assessment Model

Chapter 5: Risk Assessment Model

5.1 Introduction

There are several submenus under the 'Risk Assessment' menu. This chapter describes the use of these submenus and associated commands for running the Risk Assessment Model. Figure 5.1 show the steps involved in executing this component of the software.

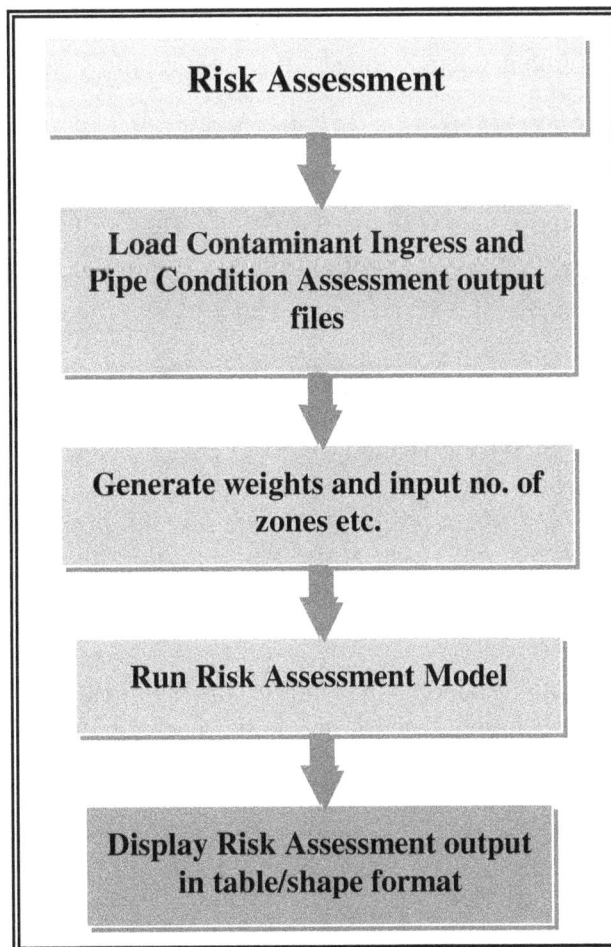

Figure 5.1. Overview of Risk Assessment Model of IRA-WDS

The following steps need to be performed in order to run the Risk Assessment Model.

- Run Model
- Display output (optional)

The example files given in Table 5.1 are to be used for illustration purposes while describing the use of the Risk Assessment Model with the help of IRA-WDS.

Table 5.1. Example input files	
Filename	**Descriptions**
Pcaoutput.out	Pipe Condition Assessment Model output
Ingressoutput.out	Ingress Model output

5.2 Running the Risk Assessment Model

The Risk Assessment Model can be run by clicking on the Tool ⬜, which is just below the 'Risk Assessment' menu or by clicking on the 'Risk Assessment' menu and then clicking on the submenu 'Run Model', as shown on the screen below:

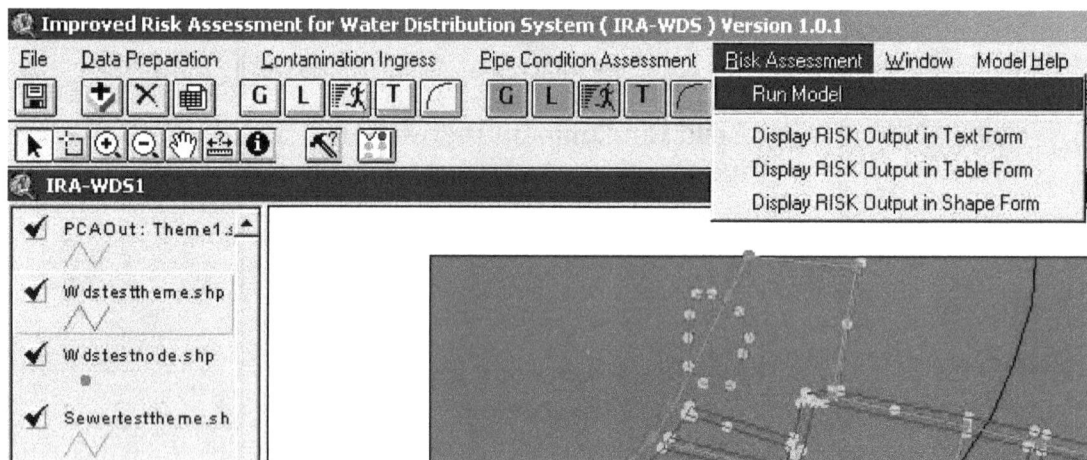

5.2.1 Loading the files

To run the Risk Assessment Model, the output files from the Contamination Ingress and Pipe Condition Assessment models are to be loaded onto the interface. To load the PCA output file, the user should click on the ⬜ button on the interface in front of the 'PCA Output File' text box. This opens the 'Load File' dialogue box, as shown on next page.

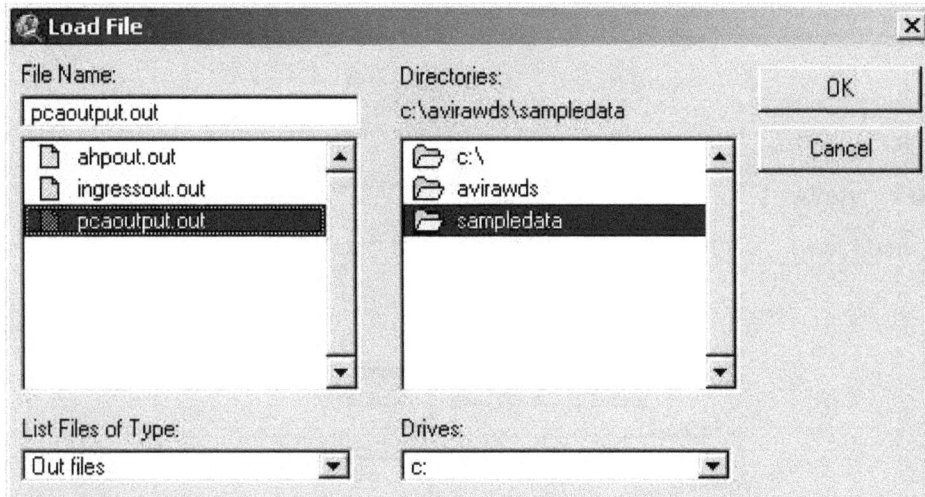

After selecting the appropriate file, the user should click on the 'OK' button; this will close the 'Load File' dialogue box and will write the name of the selected file in the 'PCA Output File' text box.

To load the Contamination Ingress output file, the user should click on the button on the interface in front of the 'Ingress Output File' text box. This opens the 'Load File' dialogue box, as shown below:

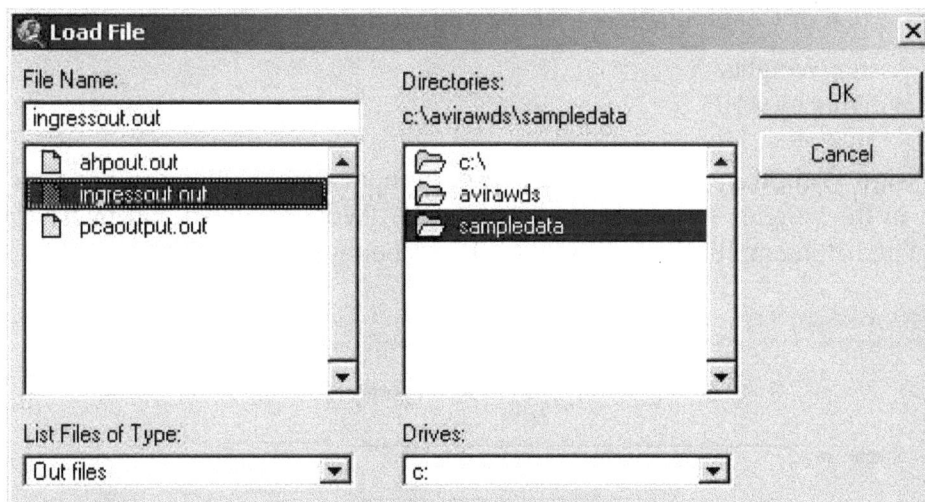

After selecting the appropriate file, the user should click on the 'OK' button; this will close the 'Load File' dialogue box and will write the name of selected file in the 'Ingress Output File' text box.

After selection of the output files from the Pipe Condition Assessment and Contamination Ingress models, the interface will look as shown on next page.

5.2.2 Weights

The 'Risk Assessment Input Form' has two options for giving importance to the Risk Assessment parameters ('Pipe Condition', 'Length of Contamination' and 'Concentration of Contamination'). These options are:

1. Assign Weights
2. Weights by AHP

The **'Assign Weights'** option allows the user to input weights directly. The user needs to type in the weights in the text box below the 'Weights' label and in front of the 'Hazard and Vulnerability' text boxes, as shown below:

The 'Weights by AHP' option allows the user to perform a pair-wise comparison and generate the weights using AHP. In this case, the user needs to enter pair-wise comparison values for the 'Hazard and Vulnerability' text boxes as shown below:

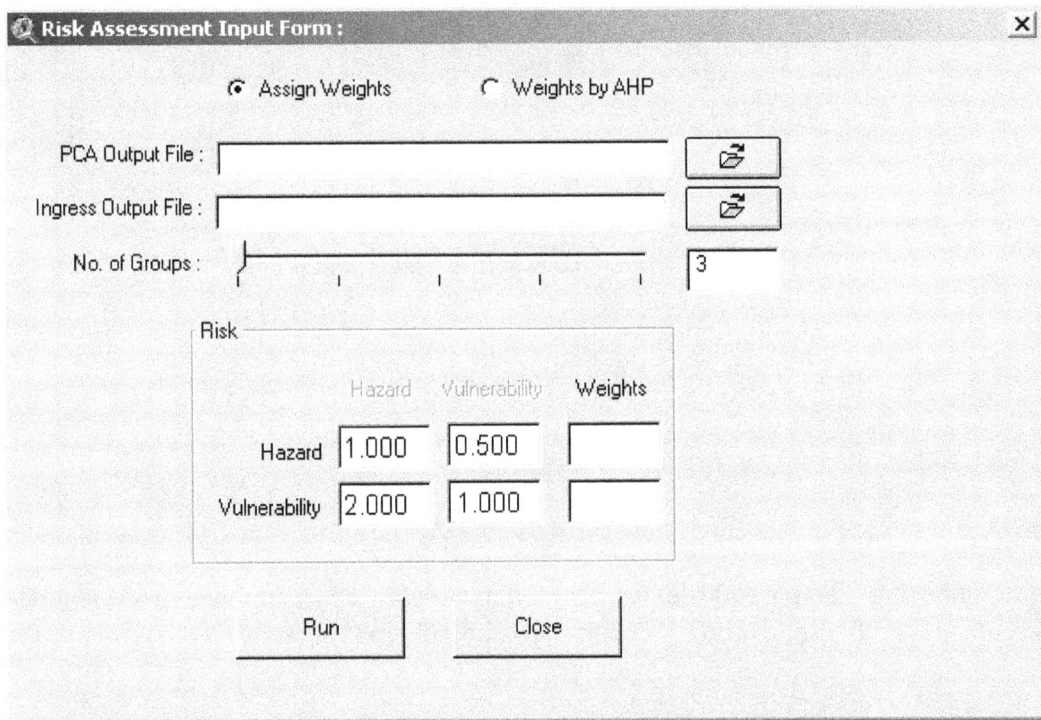

The interface also allows the user to select the number of groups in which the risk is to be categorized by sliding the bar in front of 'No. of Groups' on the 'Risk Assessment Input Form' or by entering the number of groups in the box provided, as shown above.

5.2.3 Running the Risk Model

To run the risk model, the user should click on the ⸺ Run ⸺ button on the 'Risk Assessment Input Form'. If 'Weights by AHP' has been selected, the model first writes the AHP input file for generating the weights. It then opens the 'Save AHP Input File' dialogue box to save the AHP input file generated, as shown below:

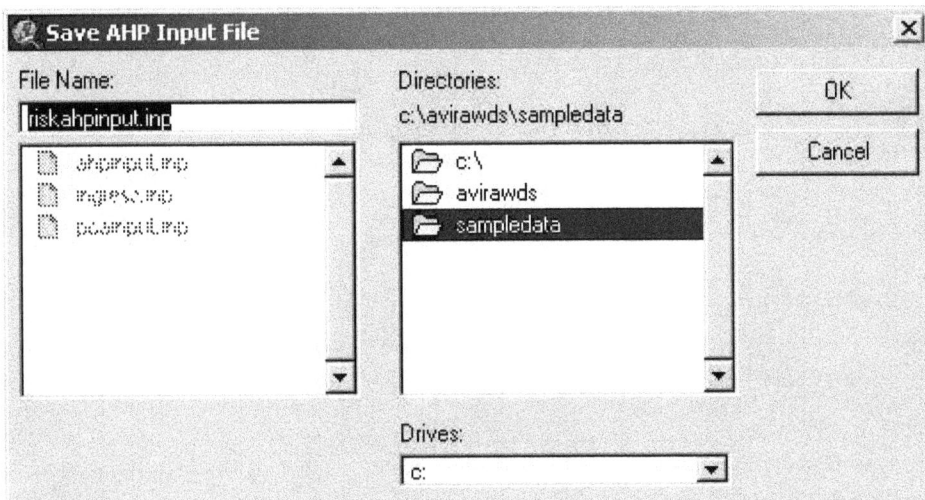

After the user clicks on the 'OK' button on the 'Save AHP Input File' dialogue box, the program runs the AHP model and opens the 'Save Risk AHP Output File' dialogue box, as shown below:

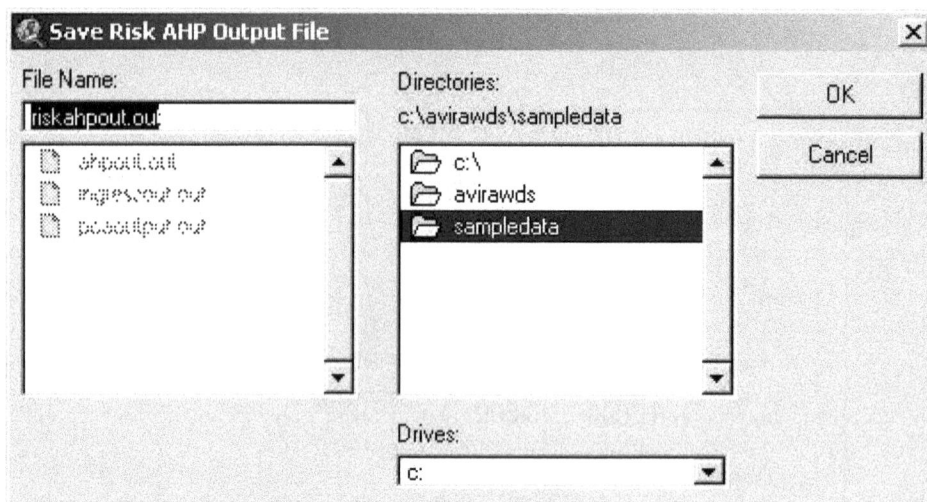

After choosing the output file to write, the weights are generated and generated weights are written in text box 'Weights' as shown below:

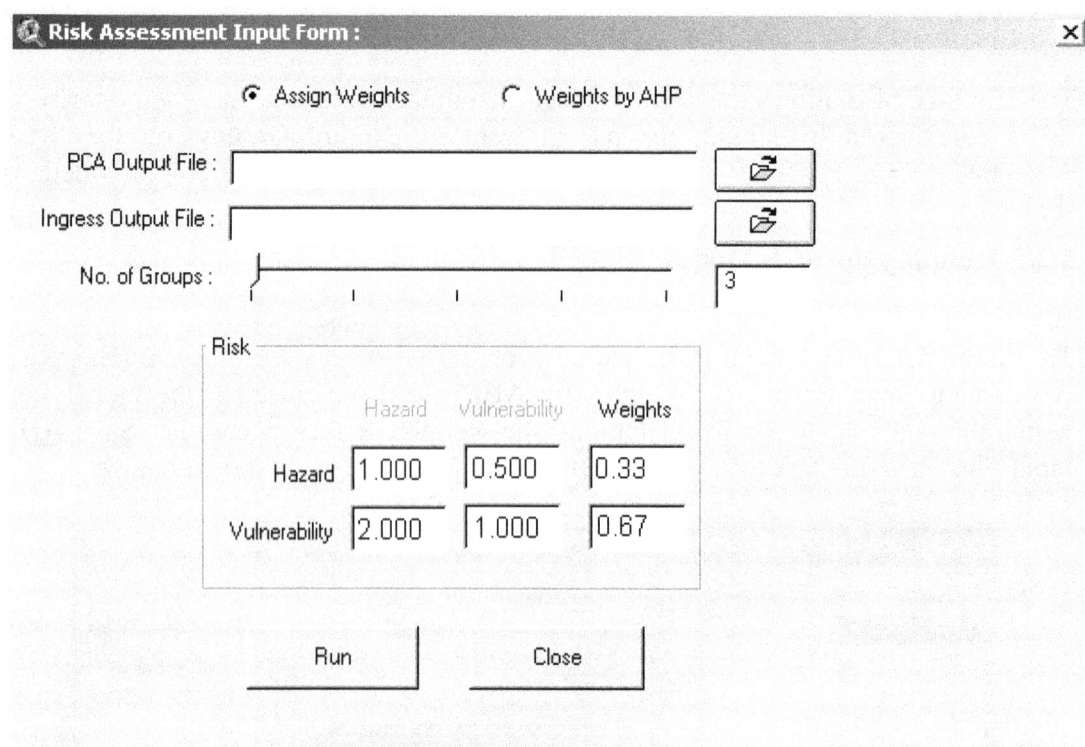

If the weights so generated are not consistent, then '–99 will' be displayed in the weights box. In this case, the user should change the matrix of 'Hazard and Vulnerability' and run the model once again.

If '**Assign Weights**' is selected the above-mentioned steps are not performed, the program opens the 'Save RISK Output File' dialogue box; this asks the user to input the filename to 'Save Risk Output File', as shown below:

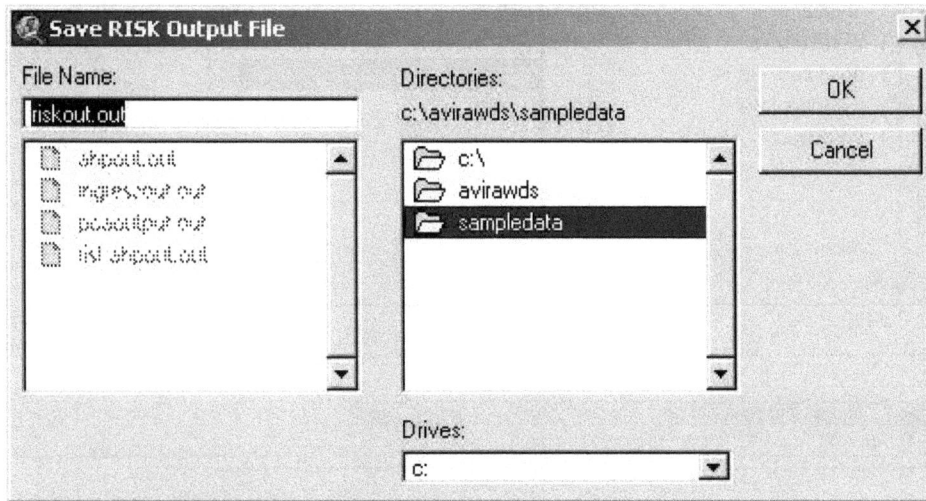

It then runs the Risk Assessment model and writes it to the file specified by the user. After completion, the program displays the 'Task Completed' Result message box, as shown below:

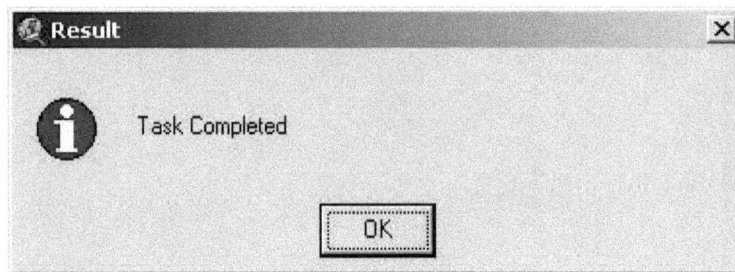

The user should click on OK to complete the task.

5.3 Displaying output

The output can be displayed in following three forms:
1. Display RISK Output in Text form
2. Display RISK Output in Table form
3. Display RISK Output in Shape form

5.3.1 Displaying Risk output in text form

The user can view the output file in text form in notepad by clicking on the [T] button or by selecting the 'Display RISK Output in Text Form' submenu from the 'Risk Assessment' menu and browsing the appropriate output file to view.

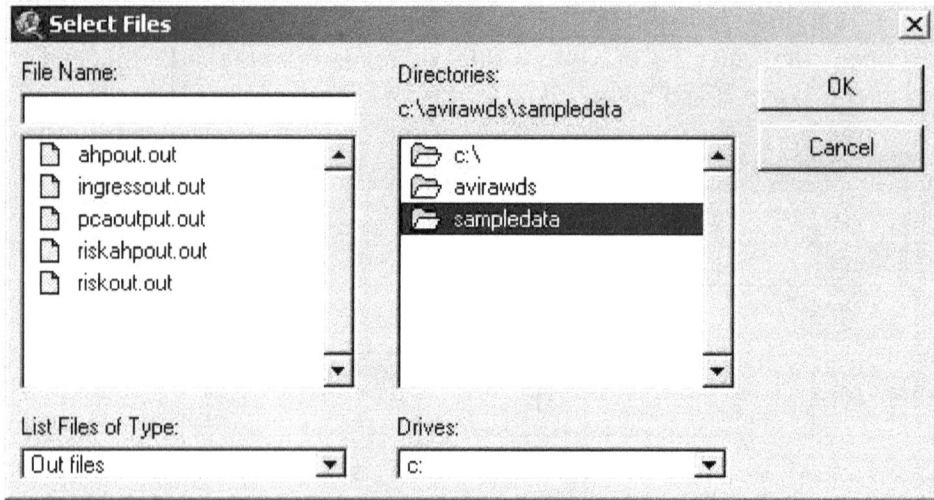

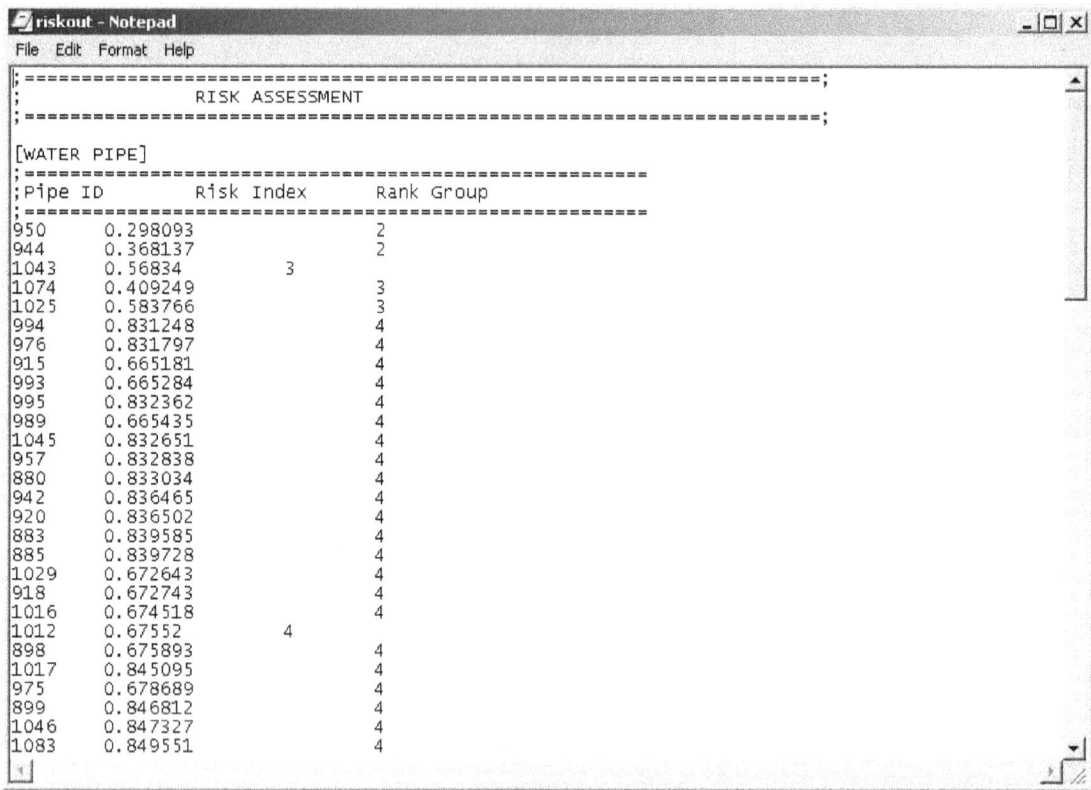

5.3.2 Displaying Risk output in table form

The user can view the output file in table form by selecting the 'Display RISK Output in Table Form' submenu from the 'Risk Assessment' menu and specifying the appropriate output file to view by browsing, as shown on next page.

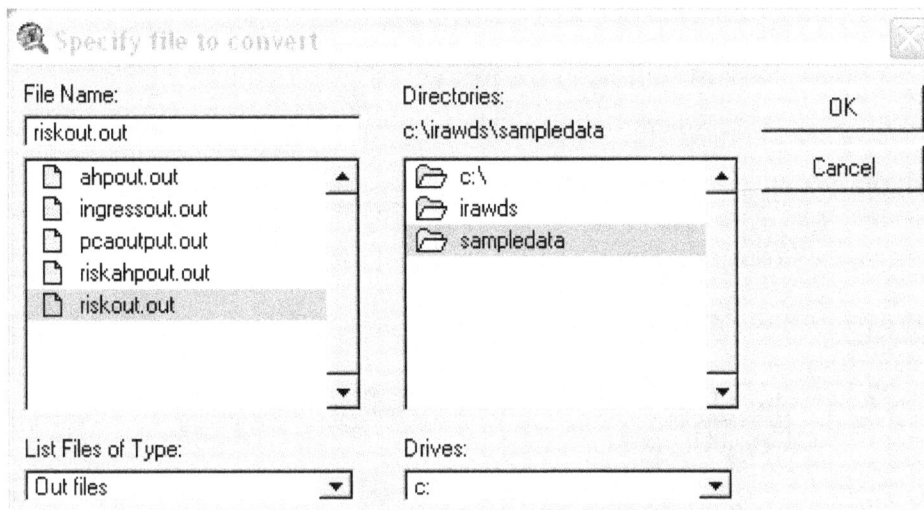

Specify file to convert

File Name:

riskout.out

- ahpout.out
- ingressout.out
- pcaoutput.out
- riskahpout.out
- riskout.out

List Files of Type:

Out files

Directories:

c:\irawds\sampledata

- c:\
- irawds
- sampledata

Drives:

c:

OK

Cancel

---

c:\irawds\sampledata\riskout.dbf

PipeID	RiskIndex	Rank
950	0.336	2
944	0.430	3
1043	0.810	4
1074	0.485	3
1025	0.830	4
831	0.925	5
975	0.594	3
824	0.926	5
880	0.927	5
852	0.931	5
866	0.932	5
837	0.932	5
951	0.932	5
936	0.602	4
1083	0.933	5
957	0.933	5
809	0.603	4
989	0.604	4
883	0.935	5
994	0.935	5
945	0.935	5
956	0.935	5
915	0.605	4
786	0.605	4
885	0.937	5
1017	0.938	5
949	0.938	5
855	0.607	4
976	0.939	5
856	0.939	5
993	0.608	4
1016	0.608	4
995	0.939	5
1045	0.940	5
1012	0.609	4
800	0.941	5
918	0.610	4
803	0.942	5
898	0.611	4
1029	0.612	4

5.3.3 Displaying Risk output in shape form

To view the Risk Assessment output in shape file form, the user should click on the ⌐ button, which is just below the 'Risk Assessment' menu or he or she should click on the 'Risk Assessment' menu and then click on the submenu 'Display RISK Output in Shape Form', as shown on the screen below:

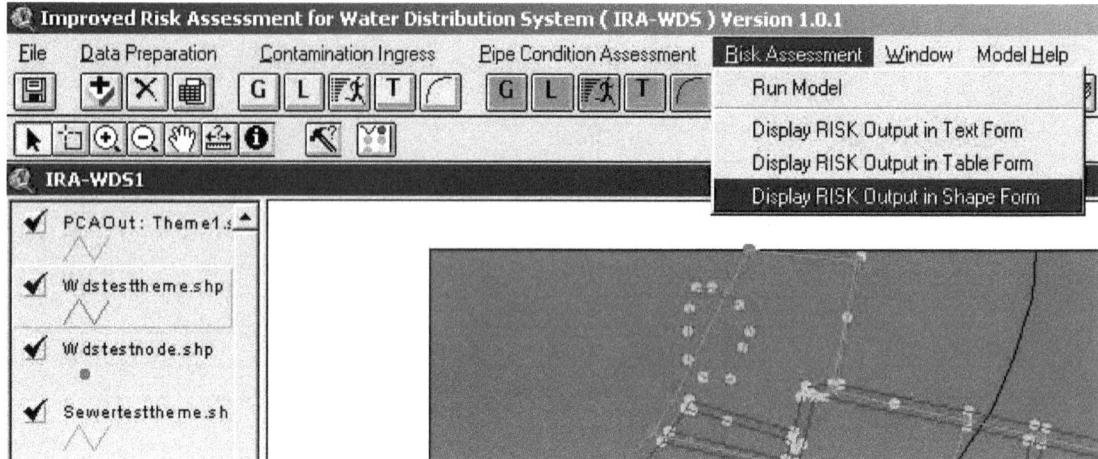

This opens the 'Display Theme' message box asking the user to specify which theme represents the water distribution system pipe theme, as shown below:

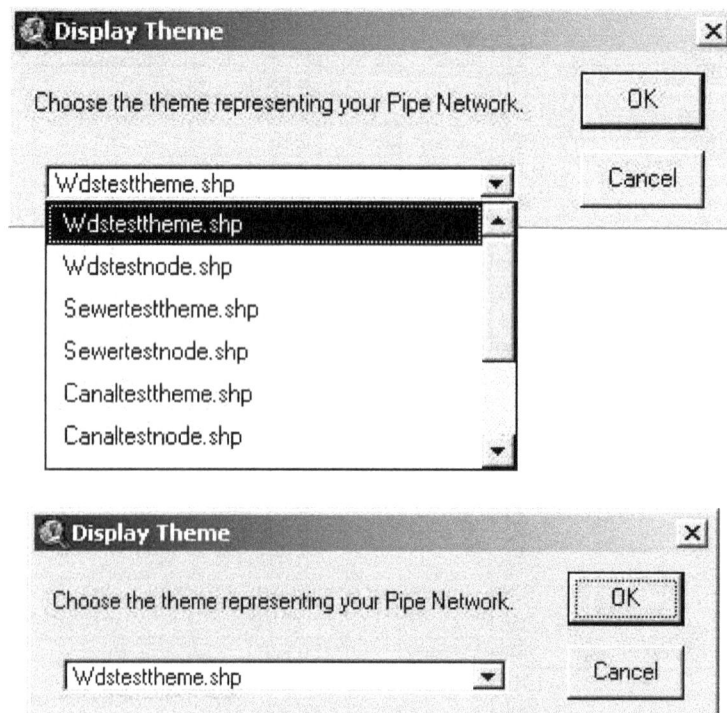

Once the user has selected the appropriate theme representing the water distribution system pipe network and has clicked on the 'OK' button, the 'Convert Theme' dialogue box appears on the screen; this asks the user to give the name with which he or she wants to store or convert the selected theme, as shown on next page.

100

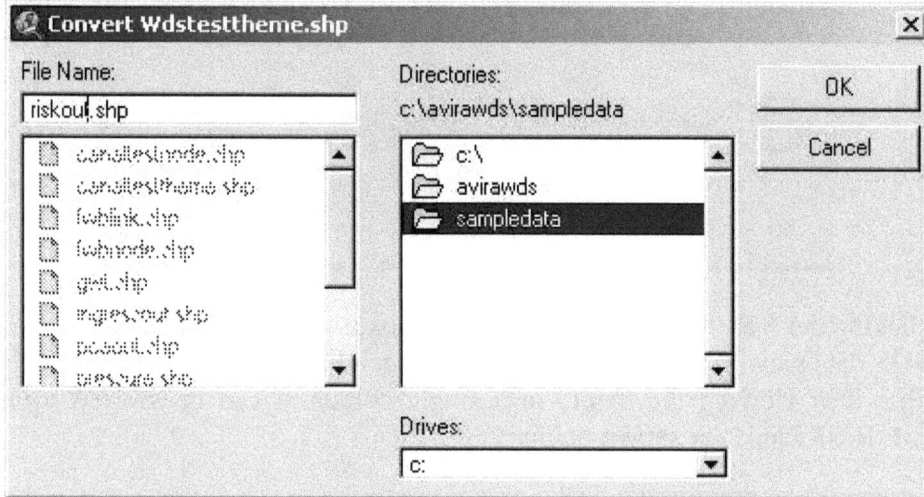

The program then opens the 'File Select' dialogue box for selecting the Risk Assessment output file as *.out, from which attributes for 'Risk Index' (RISKIndex and RISKRank) are to be added to the output theme, as shown below:

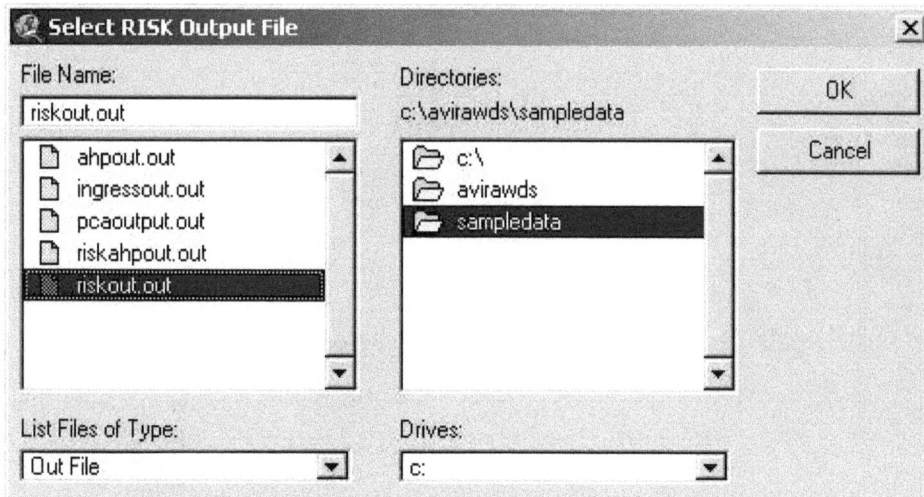

Once the user has selected the appropriate filename and clicked 'OK', the program shows the progress meter, as shown below:

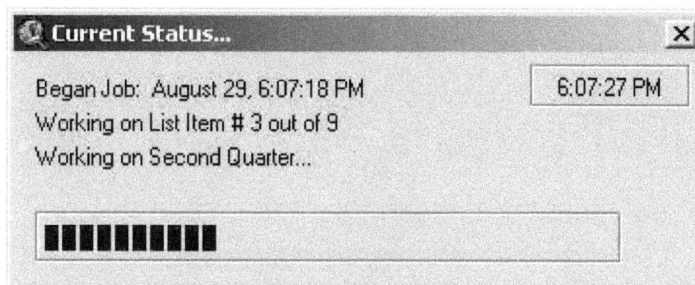

On completion of theme generation and attribute addition, it displays the ' Completed' Info message box, as shown on next page.

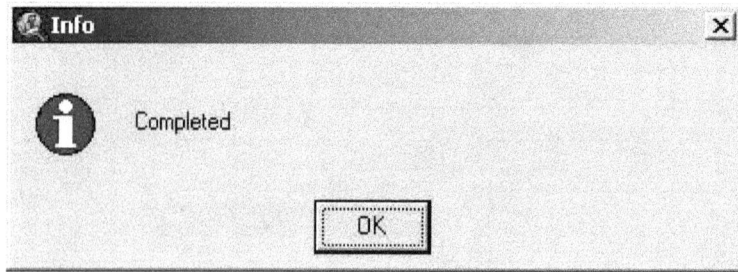

After clicking the 'OK' button on this message box, the new shape-file is added to the IRA-WDS data viewer. The 'RISKOut' theme legend needs to be changed by the user and rather than viewing the theme in a single colour, it can be viewed by unique values of 'RISKRank', as shown below:

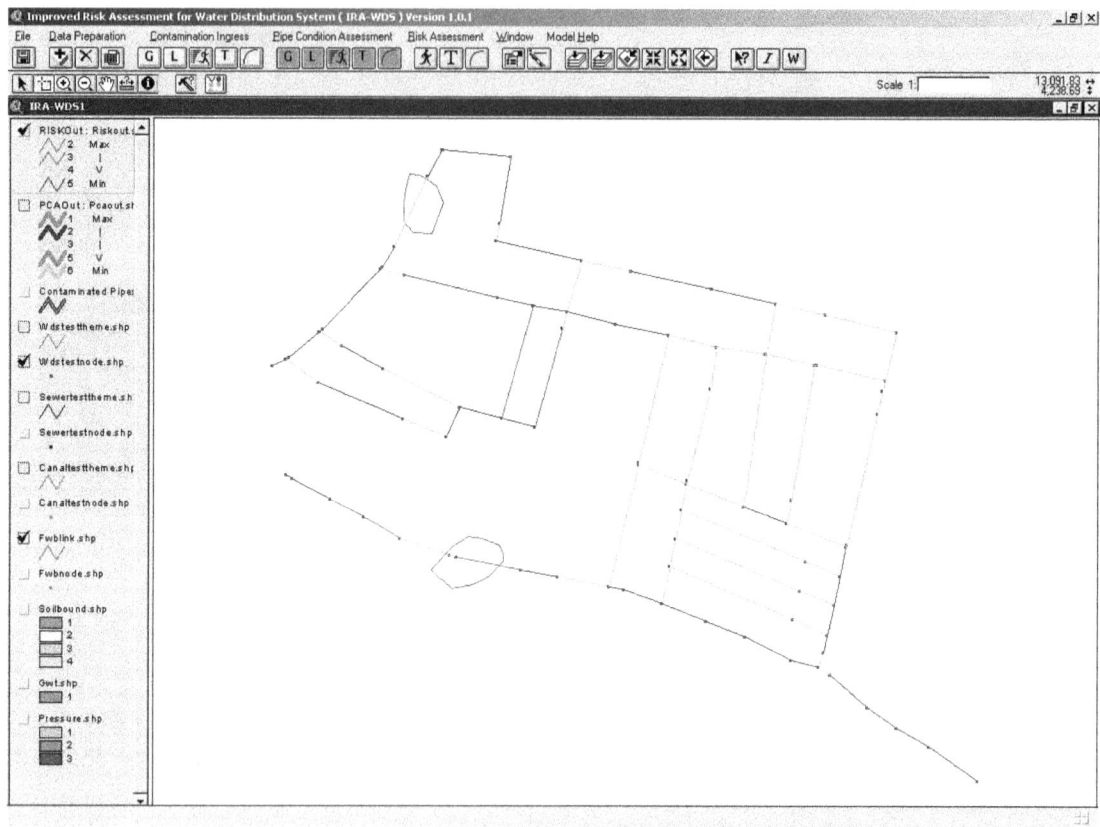

Appendix A

Inputting additional attribute data for canals and foul water bodies

1. Canals

Tables A.1. and A.2. and Figures A.1. and A.2. give details of the additional attributes required for link data and node data of canals.

Table A.1. Canal link data for Contaminant Ingress Model			
Field name	**Unit**	**Description**	**Useful references**
LINED	*Yes/No*	Lined or unlined	N/A
CROSS_SECT		Type of cross section	Section 2.3.2.1 of Book 3
TOPWIDTH	*Metres*	Top width of cross section	
BOTWIDTH	*Metres*	Bottom width of cross section	
DEPTH	*Metres*	Depth of cross section	
SEEP_RATE	*Metre/day*	Seepage rate from canal	

Table A.2. Canal node data for Contaminant Ingress Model			
Field name	**Unit**	**Description**	**Useful references**
ELEVATION	*Metres*	Elevation of the node	Section 2.3.2.1 of Book 3
WATER_DEPT	*Metres*	Depth of water in canal	

2. Foul water bodies

Table A.3. and Figure A.3. give details of the additional attributes required for node data of foul water bodies.

Table A.3. Foul water body node data for Contaminant Ingress Model			
Field name	**Unit**	**Description**	**Useful references**
WATER_DEP	*Metres*	Depth of water in water body	Section 2.3.2.2 of Book 3

ID	STARTNODE	ENDNODE	LENGTH	LINED	CROSS_SECT	TOPWIDTH	BOTWIDTH	DEPTH	SEEP_RATE
600	2306	2192	39.489	Yes	Rectangular	0.300000	0.000000	0.300000	0.050000
601	2823	2809	6.713	Yes	Rectangular	0.300000	0.000000	0.300000	0.050000
602	2840	2823	5.147	Yes	Rectangular	0.300000	0.000000	0.300000	0.050000
603	2822	2840	10.978	No	Rectangular	1.500000	0.000000	1.000000	0.000000
617	2459	2467	5.095	No	Rectangular	1.000000	0.000000	1.000000	0.000000
618	2467	2468	1.019	No	Rectangular	1.000000	0.000000	1.000000	0.000000
619	2468	2505	24.178	No	Rectangular	1.000000	0.000000	1.000000	0.000000
709	2010	2003	4.044	Yes	Rectangular	0.300000	0.000000	0.500000	0.050000
710	2063	2047	6.081	Yes	Rectangular	0.300000	0.000000	0.500000	0.050000
711	2047	2010	13.706	Yes	Rectangular	0.300000	0.000000	0.500000	0.050000
712	2134	2116	6.940	Yes	Rectangular	0.300000	0.000000	0.500000	0.050000
713	2116	2063	28.294	Yes	Rectangular	0.300000	0.000000	0.500000	0.050000
714	2184	2134	24.821	Yes	Rectangular	0.300000	0.000000	0.500000	0.050000
715	2242	2184	32.572	Yes	Rectangular	0.300000	0.000000	0.500000	0.050000
716	2263	2242	8.903	Yes	Rectangular	0.300000	0.000000	0.500000	0.050000
735	2061	2065	6.189	Yes	Rectangular	0.300000	0.000000	0.300000	0.050000
736	1998	2040	69.836	Yes	Rectangular	0.300000	0.000000	0.300000	0.050000
737	2040	2058	30.164	Yes	Rectangular	0.300000	0.000000	0.300000	0.050000
738	2058	2061	1.299	Yes	Rectangular	0.300000	0.000000	0.300000	0.050000
739	2069	2064	5.526	Yes	Rectangular	0.300000	0.000000	0.500000	0.050000
740	2064	2045	32.241	Yes	Rectangular	0.300000	0.000000	0.500000	0.050000
743	2103	2069	68.219	Yes	Rectangular	0.300000	0.000000	0.500000	0.050000
746	2108	2103	6.200	Yes	Rectangular	0.300000	0.000000	0.500000	0.050000
747	2126	2108	32.297	Yes	Rectangular	0.300000	0.000000	0.500000	0.050000
750	2132	2126	4.800	Yes	Rectangular	0.300000	0.000000	0.500000	0.050000
751	2164	2132	48.366	Yes	Rectangular	0.300000	0.000000	0.500000	0.050000
752	2156	2065	33.373	Yes	Rectangular	0.300000	0.000000	0.300000	0.050000
753	2168	2141	31.690	Yes	Rectangular	0.300000	0.000000	0.500000	0.050000
754	2170	2168	6.504	Yes	Rectangular	0.300000	0.000000	0.500000	0.050000
755	2141	2138	5.786	Yes	Rectangular	0.300000	0.000000	0.500000	0.050000
756	2138	2130	19.876	Yes	Rectangular	0.300000	0.000000	0.500000	0.050000
757	2124	2112	22.112	Yes	Rectangular	0.300000	0.000000	0.500000	0.050000
758	2130	2124	4.500	Yes	Rectangular	0.300000	0.000000	0.500000	0.050000
759	2112	2109	7.466	Yes	Rectangular	0.300000	0.000000	0.500000	0.050000
760	2230	2233	5.313	Yes	Rectangular	0.300000	0.000000	0.500000	0.050000
761	2230	2140	31.265	Yes	Rectangular	0.300000	0.000000	0.500000	0.050000
762	2233	2277	47.234	Yes	Rectangular	0.300000	0.000000	0.500000	0.050000
763	2134	2248	100.000	Yes	Rectangular	0.300000	0.000000	0.500000	0.050000

Figure A.1. Link data entry for canals

PIPEID	X_CORRD	Y_COORD	Z_COORD	ELEVATION	WATER_DEPT
1979	13314.038000	4326.405000	20.120001	20.120001	0.240000
1981	13310.040000	4326.059000	20.120001	20.120001	0.240000
1986	13297.233000	4324.951000	20.150000	20.150000	0.240000
1997	13301.232000	4320.285000	20.150000	20.150000	0.320000
1998	13306.861000	4320.182000	20.140001	20.140001	0.240000
1999	13295.048000	4320.105000	20.170000	20.170000	0.400000
2003	13241.460000	4318.540000	20.240000	20.240000	0.400000
2010	13239.854000	4314.828000	20.220001	20.220001	0.400000
2013	13376.041000	4313.977000	20.420000	20.420000	0.240000
2015	13242.506000	4313.818000	20.230000	20.230000	0.400000
2029	13259.170000	4308.878000	20.280001	20.280001	0.400000
2038	13408.004000	4306.835000	19.980001	19.980001	0.240000
2040	13375.331000	4306.434000	20.449999	20.449999	0.240000
2045	13414.221000	4305.364000	19.990002	19.990002	0.240000
2047	13231.565000	4303.913000	20.180000	20.180000	0.400000
2048	13232.246000	4303.781000	20.180000	20.180000	0.400000
2049	13291.261000	4303.485000	20.289999	20.289999	0.400000
2058	13404.767000	4299.846000	19.960001	19.960001	0.240000
2060	13290.338000	4299.639000	20.320000	20.320000	0.320000
2061	13406.034000	4299.563000	19.940001	19.940001	0.240000
2063	13227.888000	4299.070000	20.170000	20.170000	0.400000
2064	13445.794000	4298.835000	19.990000	19.990000	0.400000
2065	13412.074000	4298.211000	20.000002	20.000002	0.400000
2066	13296.128000	4298.117000	20.330000	20.330000	0.320000
2069	13451.193000	4297.662000	20.010000	20.010000	0.400000
2078	13444.176000	4291.501000	20.030001	20.030001	0.400000
2084	13287.697000	4290.278000	20.390001	20.390001	0.400000
2087	13293.581000	4289.088000	20.430000	20.430000	0.400000
2090	13300.322000	4287.692000	20.490002	20.490002	0.400000
2098	13287.668000	4285.647000	20.440001	20.440001	0.400000
2100	13315.684000	4284.511000	20.710003	20.710003	0.400000
2103	13517.854000	4283.167000	20.230000	20.230000	0.400000
2108	13523.893000	4281.761000	20.200001	20.200001	0.400000
2109	13307.285000	4281.043000	20.630001	20.630001	0.400000
2112	13314.554000	4279.337000	20.770000	20.770000	0.400000
2113	13341.776000	4279.067000	21.180002	21.180002	0.400000
2116	13209.078000	4277.934000	20.379999	20.379999	0.400000
2119	13509.846000	4277.221000	20.320002	20.320002	0.400000

Figure A.2. Node data entry for canals

	A	B	C	D	E
1	ID	X_CORRD	Y_COORD	Z_COORD	WATER_DEP
2	76	13289.500	4108.500	22.590	0.500
3	77	13300.500	4106.720	22.530	0.500
4	78	13314.000	4101.690	22.470	0.500
5	79	13277.300	4100.020	22.750	0.500
6	80	13316.600	4095.650	22.490	0.500
7	81	13316.200	4090.520	22.520	0.500
8	82	13261.800	4084.040	23.070	0.500
9	83	13305.100	4079.250	22.670	0.500
10	84	13267.400	4078.040	23.080	0.500
11	85	13271.000	4076.200	23.060	0.500
12	86	13293.300	4073.100	22.800	0.500
13	87	13277.500	4070.190	23.020	0.500
14	134	13244.200	4371.900	21.680	0.300
15	135	13252.200	4371.620	21.640	0.300
16	136	13265.300	4363.270	21.580	0.300
17	137	13241.400	4361.690	21.680	0.300
18	138	13240.400	4351.170	21.670	0.300
19	139	13270.100	4351.040	21.540	0.300
20	140	13267.100	4343.680	21.540	0.300
21	141	13240.000	4337.500	21.650	0.300
22	142	13247.500	4329.360	21.610	0.300
23	143	13261.300	4328.610	21.560	0.300

Figure A.3. Node data entry for foul water bodies

Appendix B

Time required for steady conditions

The time required for flow to establish steady conditions is determined by Philip's Equation (Philip, 1969) (B1) as being approximately equal to:

$$t_0 = \frac{5S^2}{2K_s^2}$$

(B1)

where
S – sorptivity (L/T^2)
K$_s$ – saturated hydraulic conductivity.

The estimated time to establish steady flow conditions is given in Table B.1.

Table B.1. Steady flow conditions	
Soil texture	**Time (hours)**
Sand	0.08
Loamy sand	0.50
Sandy loam	1.00
Silt loam	35.50
Loam	11.50
Sandy clay loam	6.93
Silt clay loam	38.50
Clay loam	55.50
Sandy clay	12.25
Silty clay	63.50
Clay	50.50

Reference

Philip, J. R. (1969) Theory of Infiltration. *Advances in Hydro Sciences*, Vol 5, pp 215-290.

www.ingramcontent.com/pod-product-compliance
Lightning Source LLC
Chambersburg PA
CBHW080901030426
42336CB00016B/2977